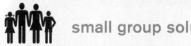

small group sol

MW01014925

13

VERY AWESOME
PROMISES

and How God Always Keeps Them

Standard
PUBLISHING

Cincinnati, Ohio

Published by Standard Publishing, Cincinnati, Ohio
www.standardpub.com

Printed in: United States of America
Editor: Lynn Lusby Pratt
Cover design: Scott Ryan
Interior design: Andrew Quach

ISBN 978-0-7847-3359-2

17 16 15 14 13 12   1 2 3 4 5 6 7 8 9

"The LORD always keeps his promises; he is gracious in all he does" (Psalm 145:13).

Contents

About These Sessions

First—thanks. Thanks for caring about children and for helping your kids discover God's awesome promises in these 13 sessions.

So have fun! You'll wow your kids with all the creative ways in which God keeps his word, and you'll equip them to trust God's promises—and to keep their own.

Welcome to Easy

These sessions make your life easy. They're light on supplies, quick to prepare, and long on fun. Because you don't have a lot of time each week to shop for supplies for crafts and object lessons, suggested supplies are common household items—things you probably already have in your kitchen, office, or garage. And because these sessions are created so beginning teachers or mature teenagers can be successful, no trained teachers are required! Because of the variety of options in each session, you can hold the attention of first graders through sixth graders. And even better, you'll help them discover truths about God!

Welcome to Simple Learning

Preparation is easy too. Each week you'll focus on one key point, one key Bible truth you want children to remember and apply in their daily lives. You'll drive home the point through Bible exploration, discussion, games, and activities that engage kids in multiple ways through multiple learning styles.

Welcome to Deep Bible Discovery

Each week your children will actually experience a Bible story in active, fun ways. Plus they'll discuss and apply what they learn. If that's what you're looking for—for your children to *do* God's Word instead of just hear it—you're in the right place. You may wish to choose a kid-friendly Bible version to help your kids understand God's Word even more. And check out the extra resources on page 112 that will further help kids experience the Bible stories!

Welcome to Flexibility

Use these 45-minute sessions with kids wherever you find them. In Sunday school, during a second service, or while kids' parents are attending an adult class or small group. And if you're leading a house church, church plant, or using other building settings where Sunday school attendance is uncertain, these sessions are for you. They're . . .

- **Multi-aged**—suitable for mixed ages of elementary children
- **Easily adapted**—sessions work for 1 or 2 kids, 12 kids, or more
- **Relational**—children grow close to Jesus *and* each other
- **Stretchable**—brimming with options to fit varying time frames
- **Fun**—even easily distracted kids can engage, learn, and grow

Use These Sessions During Adult Small Groups

Not every parent looks forward to small group as a way to get out of the house and away from the kids. For many parents, leaving kids behind is precisely what they want to avoid.

"My kids are in school all day," says Sheila, a working mother of young children. "Why would I hire a babysitter so I can be away from them in the evening? For a church event that's supposed to make my family *stronger*? Besides, have you priced babysitters lately?"

13 Very Awesome Promises and How God Always Keeps Them provides adult small groups with something fun, biblically solid, and purposeful for elementary-age kids to do while the adults are meeting. Some parents who do small groups instead of Sunday school may have children who don't attend Sunday school. This time would actually take the place of Sunday school for them. But even children who attend Sunday school will enjoy these active sessions. Here's how it works:

1. When the adult group begins, take children aside.

You'll need one adult or teenage leader to facilitate the Awesome Promises session. Ask adult small group members to take turns, or if you hire a babysitter anyway, consider paying a teenage volunteer leader from your children's ministry to lead the session. Have kids go to a different room than where adults meet. These sessions are fun—so they're sometimes loud!

2. Enjoy the session.

Relax! Each Awesome Promises session lasts about 45 minutes, with time-stretchers that easily fill another 15–30 minutes with on-target, Bible-point related activities. If the adult meeting goes long, you're ready!

3. Each week, the Howzitgoin' activity guarantees that you'll connect with kids.

It only takes a few minutes, but having children check in at the beginning of the session gives you valuable insights into what's happening in the lives of your kids. (Younger children will begin to open up after a few meetings and grow as they learn to express themselves and their feelings.)

4. Return children to their parents for prayer.

Most adult small groups and classes end with prayer. Consider bringing children back to their parents before the prayer time begins so kids can see their parents pray, watch other Christian adults turn to God, and hear how God answers prayers. Check with the adult group before bringing kids to join in!

Notice that parents get their "grown-up time" to meet with peers, yet they can still bring their kids to small group or class. And while parents are engaged in age-appropriate activities and study, so are the kids.

Even better: while the adults are forming closer relationships with each other and Jesus, so are the children!

Use These Sessions in Your Children's Ministry

All the same benefits already mentioned still apply—Awesome Promises sessions are easy to prepare, easy to teach, and connect with children in ways that make learning stick—which makes these 13 sessions perfect for a second service, a Sunday school class, or any other setting where leaders look to help children grow in their faith!

So dive in—and encourage your kids to place their faith in a God who has never broken a promise—and *never* will!

God's Promise
to His People

The Point: Nothing is too hard for God to do.
Scripture Connect: Exodus 6:1-8; 13:17, 18; 14:21-31

Supplies for all Session 1 activities options: pencils, prepared poster, paper, 2 rolls of pennies, metal spoons (2 per child), Bible, several coins, 1 plate, bucket of water, lightweight objects (see instructions)

The Basics for Leaders

God's promise: that he'd free his people. People who'd been slaves for hundreds of years, who were trapped within the borders of a superpower whose armies were more than able to keep them from escaping.

And to pry loose those thousands of enslaved people, God sent . . . one guy: Moses.

Well, Moses and Aaron. Two guys. Not great odds.

But with God, nothing is too hard. God kept his promise to his people, and he's keeping his awesome promises to his people still.

As you experience this session with your kids, consider whether you really believe that nothing is too hard for God. Because if that's true—and if God loves you—what might you ask his help with this week?

Ask him . . . and believe that God can do the impossible.

OPENING ACTIVITY—OPTION 1

HOWZITGOIN'

Time: about 5 minutes, depending on attendance
Supplies: pencils, prepared poster

Before kids arrive, draw a line on a poster. Place a 1 on the left end of the line, a 10 on the right, and a 5 in the middle. As kids arrive, ask them to pencil in their initials on the line.

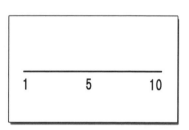

Say: **If this past week was so awful you wish you'd slept through it, place your initials by the 1. If it was a great** week you wish you could repeat, put your initials by the 10. Place your initials anywhere on the line that shows how you feel about this past week—except exactly on the 5. That's because there's no such thing as a week that's exactly half good and half bad!

After kids have signed in, give them 30 seconds each to explain why they placed their initials where they did. Be sure to include your own initials and explain your placement on the line. Kids will begin to express themselves more over time—and hearing their stories will help you adapt this lesson to make it relevant to your kids' lives.

OPENING ACTIVITY—OPTION 2

FAVORITE PLACE POSTCARDS

Time: about 10 minutes
Supplies: paper, pencils

Give children a sheet of paper and pencil. Tell them the paper is a large postcard, but instead of the card already showing a photo, they'll draw a picture of a favorite place.

Say: **You can draw a favorite place you've been or one you'd like to visit. As for me, I'll draw . . .**

Briefly share a favorite place you've visited or would like to visit, and then ask kids to draw a favorite place of their own.

Allow several minutes for kids to draw. Then ask them each to show the group what they drew and briefly talk about the place they'd like to visit.

As a group, discuss:

▪ *What is it about the place you drew that makes it a favorite place?*

▪ *If you could go tomorrow, who—if anyone—would you take with you?*

▪ *What's keeping you from going to your favorite place?*

Say: **God's people had a favorite place in mind too. They were slaves in Egypt, but God had promised them a land of their own. That was their favorite place, but to get there they needed God to rescue them from their enemies, the Egyptians. We'll talk more about that in a few minutes. But first let's play a game together!**

Awesome Promise Game

Penny Horseshoes
Time: about 10 minutes
Supplies: 2 rolls of pennies

(Note: Rolls of pennies are readily available at banks. Larger retail stores may also be willing to swap two rolls of pennies for $1, if you make a purchase.)

Before children arrive, break open one roll of pennies so the coins are loose. Place the other roll out of sight.

Ask children to stand in an open area. Give each child two pennies and these instructions: Children will toss, flip, or roll one penny at least ten feet away. Once the first penny lands, children will toss, flip, or roll their second pennies with the goal of having the second penny end up touching the first penny. It seems simple—until you try it.

Have kids play three times, getting one point if the second penny is less than a penny-width from the first penny and two points if the pennies are touching.

Give each child an additional penny and have kids play with the same rules but with three pennies. Play several rounds.

Say: **You're doing well, but if you'd like to see how it's really done, watch me. I can do it with fifty pennies. And they'll *all* be touching!**

Expect scoffing, until you produce the roll of pennies and roll it to where their pennies are scattered on the floor. Then expect cries of "That's cheating!"

Ask kids to collect pennies and give them to you. Then, as a group, discuss:

▪ *What made this game easy or hard?*

▪ *Tell about a time you tried to do something you thought would be easy—but it turned out to be hard.*

▪ *What's something hard to do that you need help doing?*

▪ *What's something hard to do that you need* God's *help doing?*

Say: **We're going to talk about something that God's people needed God's help doing: getting out of slavery. They'd been slaves in Egypt for 400 years, and the Egyptian king, Pharaoh, didn't want to let them go. But unless they got away, they couldn't go to the promised land. God promised to help them. Let's hear more about that!**

Promise Kept BIBLE STORY

CLICK IT

Time: about 15 minutes
Supplies: metal spoons (2 per child), Bible

Give each child two metal spoons and ask kids to hold their spoons in one hand, the bowls of the spoons back-to-back. Have kids practice moving their spoons up and down against the palms of their hands to create a clicking sound. Let kids practice for 30 seconds before you ask them to remain quiet.

Explain that the sound effect they'll be making is the sound of God's people marching out of Egypt. During the story when they hear that God's people are on the move—that's when they'll make the sound.

Read aloud Exodus 6:1-8; 13:17, 18; 14:21-31. Encourage kids to clack their spoons as you read Exodus 13:18 and 14:21-23, in particular.

When you've finished reading—and kids have clacked—collect spoons and, as a group, discuss:

• What was surprising about how God kept his promise to help his people become free and get to the promised land?

• God wanted to get his people to the promised land, but the Egyptians got in the way. What's something that God wants you to do or be—and what's in your way?

Say: **God didn't give his people an army that would fight back when the Egyptians came after them. God used water to beat the Egyptian army—and he kept his promise to help his people get to the promised land. Back then, nothing was too hard for God! And that's still true today—nothing is too hard for God to do. He's still keeping his awesome promises to us!**

CLOSING PRAYER

POWERFUL PRAYER

Time: about 5 minutes
Supplies: none

Ask kids to join you in standing in a circle. Say: **God's people found out that there's nothing too hard for God to do. Free them from slavery?**

He could do it. Help them get to the promised land? He could do that too.

When we think of God, let's think of him as powerful. Please join me in getting on our knees to worship our powerful God.

Have kids join you by getting on their knees. Thank God for his power. Then say: When we think of God, let's think of him as loving. He loves us.

Have kids imitate you as you cup your hands in front of you. Explain that you're doing this as a sign that you want to receive God's love. Thank God for his love.

Have kids join you in standing again. Say: When we think of God, let's think of him helping us stand strong on his promises. Thank God for his promises.

Finish by praying: In Jesus' name, amen.

EXTRA-TIME ACTIVITY—OPTION 1

MOVE THEM ISRAELITES!
Time: about 10 minutes
Supplies: several coins, 1 plate

Scatter coins on the floor and tell kids their job is to move the coins from the floor to the plate—without using their hands. Don't suggest alternatives; kids will quickly think to pull off their shoes and use their toes . . . or find another alternative. (Note: But don't let them use their mouths/teeth; coins could be swallowed.)

Explain that the world record for the task is 90 seconds and their job is to beat the record. Before starting the clock, have them discuss how they'll work together and accomplish the task.

Then give them 90 seconds, but allow a second 90 seconds, if necessary. As a group, discuss:

- *What made this "impossible" task easier—or harder?*
- *Tell about a time when you and some friends did something together that you couldn't have done by yourself.*

Say: **God's people—the Israelites—were like the coins: they couldn't move without help. They needed God's help to escape Egypt. It seemed impossible, but nothing is too hard for God to do! God kept his promise.**

- *What's an "impossible" thing that you'd like God to do?*

EXTRA-TIME ACTIVITY—OPTION 2

DOES IT FLOAT?
Time: about 10 minutes
Supplies: bucket of water, lightweight objects

Before children arrive, collect a variety of lightweight objects: corks, paper clips, feathers, plastic lids, pencils, buttons, rubber bands, etc.

Place the bucket of water where children can all gather around it. One at a time, drop the objects into the water, asking before each object is dropped who thinks it will sink and who thinks it will float.

Then say: **God used water to drown the Egyptian army. When the water rushed in, soldiers couldn't swim to safety. The chariots—the small wagons pulled by horses, which soldiers rode into battle—didn't float!** Discuss:

- *Why do you think God didn't just kill the Egyptian army before they got to where God's people were waiting?*
- *How has God shown his power and love to you? How has he kept you safe in scary places and during scary times?*
- *If God promises something, he'll do it. Nothing is too hard for God to do. Do you believe that? Why or why not?*

EXTRA-TIME ACTIVITY—OPTION 3

INQUIRING MINDS WANT TO KNOW

Time: about 5 minutes

Supplies: none

Gather kids in a circle. Ask: **If nothing is too hard for God, why hasn't God solved all the problems in the world, like war and hunger?**

God's Promise
to Noah

The Point: We can trust God to keep his word.
Scripture Connect: Genesis 7:17-24; 9:1-17

Supplies for all Session 2 activities options: pencils, prepared poster, watch with a second hand, shoe box, damp cloth, scissors, heavy-duty tape, old magazines and newspapers, Bible, paper, markers, glue, 3-foot lengths of string (or twine or rope; 1 per child)

The Basics for Leaders

God's promise: that never again would there be a global flood.

God made that promise to Noah, who'd just seen what a global flood could do. He'd watched everyone he knew die—except for his immediate family. He'd watched crops destroyed, villages swept away, livestock drowned.

Never again, God promised. And God even spread a rainbow across the sky as a reminder.

Noah chose to trust God—and you can trust God too. As you experience this session with your kids, you'll thank God for keeping his promise to Noah— and all his awesome promises to you.

What promises are you trusting God to keep? And what might happen if you thanked him now for keeping those promises?

OPENING ACTIVITY—OPTION 1

HOWZITGOIN'

Time: about 5 minutes, depending on attendance
Supplies: pencils, prepared poster

Before kids arrive, draw a line on a poster. Place a 1 on the left end of the line, a 10 on the right, and a 5 in the middle. As kids arrive, ask them to pencil in their initials on the line.

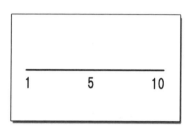

Say: **If this past week was so awful you wish you'd slept through it, place your initials by the 1. If it was a great week you wish you could repeat, put your initials by the 10. Place your initials anywhere on the line that shows how you feel about this past week—except exactly on the 5. That's because there's no such thing as a week that's exactly half good and half bad!**

After kids have signed in, give them 30 seconds each to explain why they placed their initials where they did. Be sure to include your own initials and explain your placement on the line. Kids will begin to express themselves more over time—and hearing their stories will help you adapt this lesson to make it relevant to your kids' lives.

OPENING ACTIVITY—OPTION 2

RAINBOW RACE

Time: about 10 minutes
Supplies: watch with a second hand

You'll need an open area for this activity. Ask children to pair up and stand in two rows, facing each other. Move the rows so the last pair in each row is up against a wall. If you have an odd number of children, participate yourself.

Say: **Today we'll talk about a promise God made that came with a**

built-in reminder: a rainbow. To get started, let's have a rainbow race!

Ask pairs to join hands at shoulder height and then raise their hands. Once pairs have joined hands, children will take a step back to create an arch through which other children can pass. The goal: pairs will take turns passing through the arches created by other pairs to move the entire line of kids across the room from the starting wall to the far wall. After each pair moves under the arches, it will quickly reform an arch in line, and the next pair will pass under in turn.

Do this activity twice, seeing whether kids can improve the time it takes to cross the room with every child moving through the arches. Then play again—with all arches formed while kids are on their knees. Everyone will have to crawl on hands and knees to pass under the arches.

Then have kids sit on the floor and, as a group, discuss:

- *Tell about a time you saw a real rainbow. Where was it?*
- *What do you know about rainbows?*
- *What do you think about when you see a rainbow?*

Say: **We'll look today at what God said about rainbows—and what God suggests we think about when we see one. Rainbows can remind us of a promise God made to Noah. But before we do that, let's make some promises ourselves!**

Awesome Promise Game

Touchy-Feely

Time: about 10 minutes
Supplies: shoe box, damp cloth, scissors, heavy-duty tape

Before children arrive, cut a hole in the end of the shoe box that a child's hand will fit through. Place a damp cloth in the box. (If at all possible, use a cloth that has been in a freezer.) Tape the lid closed.

Ask children to sit in a circle. Explain that you'll pass around the box and, one at a time, children are to reach inside and feel what's there. Then each child will, in turn, share one thing about what's inside the box. Explain these rules:

- **No peeking—you can feel what's inside but not look at it.**
- **No comment can reveal what's inside.**
- **Comments made can be true—or not.**
- **Every comment must end with "I promise."**

Say: **For instance, you might reach inside, pull out your hand, and say, "What's inside feels like a snake, but it won't bite you—I promise." Of course, that promise may be true—or not.**

Pass the box to your right after reaching inside while repeating the snake comment.

After the shoe box has gone all around the circle, have kids guess what's inside. Reveal what's there.

Then say: **Sometimes people make promises that aren't true. For me that was . . .**

Briefly describe a time someone made a false promise to you. Sharing a story models the sort of response you're hoping to get from the kids—and helps them know you better. Then, as a group, discuss:

- *Your turn. Tell about a time someone made a promise to you, but it wasn't true. What was the promise? How did you feel?*
- *Sometimes we don't keep promises either. How do you feel when you make a promise and then don't keep it?*

Say: **God has never made a promise he didn't keep. Let's look at a promise he made to a man named Noah—a promise God also made to you.**

Promise Kept BIBLE STORY

MONTAGE
Time: about 15 minutes
Supplies: old magazines and newspapers, Bible

Ask kids to pair up and sit on the floor, with space between pairs. Give each pair a few magazines and newspapers.

Say: **Please listen as I read these Bible passages about an event—the flooding of the earth.**

Read aloud Genesis 7:17-24; 9:1-17. Ask pairs to discuss:

AGE-ALERT TIPS

If you have very **young children,** pair them with **older kids.**

• *What part of that story did you find most interesting? Why?*

After kids talk in pairs, ask each pair to create a montage about what they found interesting. They'll use the floor as their "board." They can rip words and images out of the newspapers and magazines.

For instance, if they thought it interesting that only one family was saved, they can look for pictures and words about "one," about family, about people being saved, or about floods.

Allow time for pairs to create their art. Then have kids stand and, as a group, move from montage to montage as the creators of each montage explain what they created.

After each pair has shared, have kids move away from the montages to sit in a circle (they'll need the montages intact for use with the Thank-You Cards activity below). As a group, discuss:

• *What was easy or hard about this montage activity? Why?*

• *If you could find the perfect picture to show how you feel about God's promise to never flood the entire world again, what picture would you choose?*

• *We have floods in places on the earth these days. How sure are you that God won't just flood everything again? Why?*

Say: **We can trust God to keep his word. Let's thank him for that!**

CLOSING PRAYER

RAINBOW PROMISE PRAYER
Time: about 5 minutes
Supplies: none

Ask kids to join you in standing in a circle. Say: **If you look closely at a** rainbow, you can see seven colors: red, orange, yellow, green, blue, indigo, and violet. As a group, let's think of seven things that we can thank God for. Some of those things might even be the same colors that we can see in the rainbow. For instance, I might pray, "God, thank you for this beautiful green and blue planet where I can live." I'll start, and when we've thanked God for seven things—no matter what color they are—I'll close.

Begin by thanking God for keeping his awesome promises. If kids offer additional thoughts, great. If they don't, thank God for his love, for sending Jesus, for giving you all life, for forgiving you when you ask, for each other, and for a future with him in Heaven. Finish by praying: **In Jesus' name, amen.**

EXTRA-TIME ACTIVITY—OPTION 1

THANK-YOU CARDS

Time: about 10 minutes
Supplies: paper, markers, glue, montages created in the Montage activity

Ask kids to each choose one picture from their montages to glue on the front of a sheet of paper. Then, on the back, they can write God a thank-you note for keeping his promises—no matter what.

After kids have finished, have them take their creations home to display where they'll see them often. Say: **Let your thank-you note be a reminder: God always keeps his promises. He kept his promise to Noah—and he'll keep his promises to us!**

AGE-ALERT TIPS

Help **younger children** write their notes.

STRING SHAPES

Time: about 10 minutes

Supplies: 3-foot lengths of string (or twine or rope; 1 per child), Bible

Say: **I love that God keeps his word! Here are promises he's made that I'm trusting him to keep.** Read aloud these verses:

- **"How can a young person stay pure? By obeying your word" (Psalm 119:9).**
- **"The Lord . . . will take care of you" (Psalm 55:22).**
- **"He has removed our sins as far from us as the east is from west" (Psalm 103:12).**
- **"I will not abandon you as orphans—I will come to you" (John 14:18).**

Give each child a length of string and these instructions: **Lay your string on the ground in the shape of one of those promises of God—or another promise God has made. For instance, if one of your favorite promises is that God will let you live with him in Heaven, create the shape of a gate or a giant *H*.**

Allow kids time to shape their creations and then, as a group, see if you can guess what each shape means.

As a group, discuss:

- *God promised to never again flood the earth. What else has God promised never to do?*
- *What has God promised always to do?*
- *How does it feel knowing you can always count on God?*

INQUIRING MINDS WANT TO KNOW

Time: about 5 minutes

Supplies: none

Gather kids in a circle.

Ask: **God always keeps his promises to us. How well do you think you keep your promises to God? Why do you say that?**

God's Promise
to Abram

The Point: God keeps his promises—but we may have to wait.
Scripture Connect: Genesis 12:1-7; 13:14-18; 21:1-5

Supplies for all Session 3 activities options: pencils, prepared poster, paper, envelopes (1 per child), ice cubes (1 per child), paper towels, bowl in which to collect ice cubes, Bible

The Basics for Leaders

Waiting . . . That's something most of us don't do well.

To be fair, we're trained to *not* wait. We eat fast food, get fast answers from the Internet, move around in fast cars. We've forgotten how to wait.

Which means that when someone makes us a promise—we expect fast results. But when that promise comes from God, fast results aren't always part of the deal.

Just ask Abram.

God promised Abram that he'd move to a new land, have a child, and through Abram the world would be blessed. The move happened quickly. The child took 25 years.

And that big blessing? Another 40 generations, give or take.

God always keeps his promises. That's good news because God has made some promises to you too. As you experience this session with your kids, you'll have the chance to think about some of those promises.

You'll also have the chance to consider whether you really trust God to deliver on his awesome promises. Because if we take God at his word—really take him at his word—that changes how we live.

That was true for Abram . . . and it's true for you.

OPENING ACTIVITY—OPTION 1

HOWZITGOIN'

Time: about 5 minutes, depending on attendance
Supplies: pencils, prepared poster

Before kids arrive, draw a line on a poster. Place a 1 on the left end of the line, a 10 on the right, and a 5 in the middle. As kids arrive, ask them to pencil in their initials on the line.

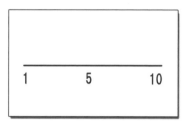

Say: **If this past week was so awful you wish you'd slept through it, place your initials by the 1. If it was a great week you wish you could repeat, put your initials by the 10. Place your initials anywhere on the line that shows how you feel about this past week—except exactly on the 5. That's because there's no such thing as a week that's exactly half good and half bad!**

After kids have signed in, give them 30 seconds each to explain why they placed their initials where they did. Be sure to include your own initials and explain your placement on the line. Kids will begin to express themselves more over time—and hearing their stories will help you adapt this lesson to make it relevant to your kids' lives.

OPENING ACTIVITY—OPTION 2

SLOOOOOOW MAIL

Time: about 10 minutes
Supplies: pencils, paper, envelopes (1 per child)

Have children get in groups of two. Give each child a sheet of paper and an envelope. Say: **You'll write a note to your partner. Please sit where your partner can't read what you're writing.**

Tell children to write encouraging, positive notes. For instance, they might describe what they like about their partner, or promise to pray for their partner.

Give children two minutes to write. Then ask kids to fold their notes, seal their notes in envelopes, and write their partners' names on the outside of their envelopes.

Have children join you in a circle. Ask partners to exchange envelopes—but not to open those envelopes.

Say: **I'll write "Do not open until** (give kids a date six months away)**" on your envelopes.** (Do so.) **Hold your envelopes as we talk.**

As a group discuss:

• *What's making it easy or hard to wait to read your note?*

Say: **Waiting can be hard, can't it? That's especially true with promises. If I promised you an amazingly cool gift on your birthday, you'd want your birthday to be tomorrow!**

One time when it was hard for me to wait for a promise to be kept was . . . Briefly share about a time you had to wait for a promise to be kept. Maybe your parents promised you a trip to Disney World, or you planned your wedding and looked forward to your wedding day. Sharing your story models what sort of story you'd like your kids to share. It also helps them get to know you better.

Say: **Your turn now. Tell about a time it was hard for you to wait for a promise to be kept. Tell what the promise was and how it felt to wait.**

Allow time for kids to share their stories. Then thank kids for sharing.

Say: **Today we'll meet someone who had to wait for promises to be kept. God made those promises to a man named Abram. Abram had to decide if he trusted God to keep his promises or not. And good news: God kept his promises to Abram . . . and God will keep his promises to you.**

Awesome Promise Game

Ice Cold Questions
Time: about 10 minutes
Supplies: ice cubes (1 per child), paper towels, bowl

Ask children to sit on the floor in a circle. Say: **I promise you, it's going to feel better. If you're wondering what I mean, I'll show you.**

Give each child an ice cube. Say: **Hold your cube in one hand—and no switching hands. Hold your ice cube as we talk about a few things. And I promise—your hand will feel better . . . sometime. Trust me!**

As a group (and while everyone holds the cubes) discuss the following—as long as possible but not until the kids are really hurting:

• *A man named Abram moved from one country to another. If you moved to a new country, what would you miss about this one?*

• *If you were to move today, what's something you have that you'd want to be sure you took with you? Why?*

• *If you've ever moved, tell about that. How long until you felt at home in your new neighborhood?*

Thank kids for sharing and give each child a paper towel. Collect melting ice cubes in the bowl and encourage kids to warm their hands. Say: **I told you you'd feel better! Promise kept—just not as quickly as you might have liked.**

Life can be like holding an ice cube. Sometimes life is "cold"—people treat us badly; life's not fair. Sometimes life is hard—we have problems. But things will get better. Many things get better right away. But things will get better someday for sure! I know that's true because God promised that if we know and love Jesus, someday we'll be with him in Heaven. And God keeps his promises—always.

Here are some awesome promises God has made to you.

Read the following passages aloud. Or even better, if you have confident readers in your group, ask children to read the passages aloud. Be sure to emphasize the points in parentheses.

1. Matthew 11:28, 29 (In Jesus you'll find comfort and rest.)
2. Romans 8:37-39 (Nothing can separate us from God's love.)
3. Romans 10:9 (You can be saved from sin.)
4. 1 John 1:9 (You can be forgiven.)
5. John 14:3 (Jesus has a place for you in Heaven.)
6. Revelation 21:3, 4 (Heaven is a place of joy—forever.)

Say: **Those are all promises God has made—to you. God made promises to Abram too. Let's see what those promises were and how God kept them.**

Promise Kept BIBLE STORY

DO THE MATH

Time: about 15 minutes
Supplies: Bible, paper, pencils

Ask kids to join you in forming a circle, seated on the floor. Give each child a sheet of paper and a pencil.

Say: **Math quiz! Please figure out the answer to this question: How long did it take God to keep his promises to Abram?**

To figure that out, you'll need to know what promises God made and how much time passed between when God made the promises and when God kept them.

Use your pencil and paper to take notes as I read passages from the Bible that contain hints. We'll work together to figure this out.

AGE-ALERT TIPS

If you have **young children,** pair them with **older ones** who can help with the math.

Read aloud Genesis 12:1-7; 13:14-18; and 21:1-5. As a group discuss:

• *What promises did God make to Abram?* (to give him a new home, to give him many descendants, to bless the world through him—Genesis 12:2, 3, 7; 13:14-16; 21:1, 2)

• *How long did it take God to keep his promises?* (new land: not long; having a son: 25 years; see below about blessing the world)

• *The "blessing the world" promise was kept when Jesus was born—he came from the family of Abram. But how long did that take? Any ideas?*

Give kids a chance to answer. Say: **We can get closer to figuring it out by looking at the book of Matthew, chapter 1. Matthew lists 42 generations between Abram and Jesus.**

Show kids the chapter in the Bible. Say: **I won't read this out loud, because the names are way hard to pronounce—like Zerubbabel! But think about it: God promised Abram that the world would be blessed through him—through his family. That happened when his grandson was born.**

Wait . . . not grandson. Great-grandson. Actually . . .

Say the word *great* 42 times, counting on your fingers, and then say *grandson*.

If each generation was 30 years, how long would that be? 42 x 30 = 1,260 years! That's a long time to wait for a promise to be kept—and it may have been longer. We don't know exactly.

When we're waiting for a promise to be kept, it's easier if we trust the person who made the promise.

As a group discuss:

- *What makes it easy for you to trust God?*
- *What makes it hard to trust God?*
- *What would make it even easier for you to trust God?*

Say: **I'm glad God always keeps his promises, even if I have to wait. Sometimes waiting for God helps me trust him more. I remember that God is in charge, and I'm not!**

CLOSING PRAYER

PATIENCE PRAYER

Time: about 5 minutes
Supplies: none

Ask kids to join you in standing in a circle. Say: **You have a friend who always keeps his promises. That friend is God. Let's take a few minutes to thank God for being so faithful. And let's thank God for those things he's promised us—because he will deliver! He'll keep his promises.**

I'll mention a promise of God and then pause. Please thank God for

his promise as I pause, and then I'll go on to the next one. You can pray out loud or quietly.

Pray: **God, thank you for loving us.** (pause) **Thank you for saving us from sin.** (pause) **Thank you for forgiving us when we sin.** (pause) **Thank you for always keeping your promises.** (pause) **Thank you for your promise that we can be with you forever in Heaven.** (pause) **In Jesus' name, amen.**

EXTRA-TIME ACTIVITY—OPTION 1

SILLY WALK CENTRAL
Time: about 10 minutes
Supplies: none

Ask kids to line up against one wall, facing the opposite wall. Say: **Abram and his family walked to their new home. Let's see how many ways you can walk.**

Ask kids to walk in a variety of ways, each time from wall to wall. (Suggestions: baby steps, giant steps, on tiptoe, like ice-skaters, running, hopping, like kangaroos "walk," like snakes "walk," like chickens walk.)

Have kids sit again and discuss:
• *What was your favorite walk—and why?*
• *Abram was walking to a new home. Show the rest of us how you'd walk if you were walking to a new home.*

Say: **Maybe Abram walked quickly with a spring in his step—he was sure God would keep his promise. Maybe, as Abram walked, he looked back over his shoulder sometimes because he missed his old home.**

Either way, he kept going. Abram trusted God's promise. We can trust God too. God always keeps his promises—even if we have to wait awhile.

EXTRA-TIME ACTIVITY—OPTION 2

COUNT OFF
Time: about 10 minutes
Supplies: none

Ask kids to stand in random spots around the room (not touching each other) and to close their eyes. Tell them that the goal is for them, as a group, to count aloud from one to ten. The kids will call out numbers—"one," "two," and so forth until someone says "ten." It seems simple, but they have to make it from one to ten without two kids calling out a number at the same time, or calling out the same number twice. If that happens, the group must start over.

The rules: no peeking and no planning!

When kids finish (and this could take a few minutes!) discuss:

• *How did you feel while doing this game? Why?*

• *You didn't know how long it would take to finish this game. Do you like not knowing when things will happen or do you like to plan ahead?*

• *God keeps his promises—but he doesn't tell us when he'll keep all of them. If you could know when God would keep just one of his promises to you, which would you choose—and why?*

EXTRA-TIME ACTIVITY—OPTION 3

INQUIRING MINDS WANT TO KNOW
Time: about 5 minutes
Supplies: none

Gather kids in a circle. Ask: *If God loves us, why doesn't he always keep his promises right away?*

God's Promise
to David

The Point: God knows the future.

Scripture Connect: 2 Samuel 23:5; 2 Chronicles 13:4, 5; Matthew 1:1, 17

Supplies for all Session 4 activities options: pencils, prepared poster, newspaper, paper, markers, tape, safety scissors (several pairs), movable furniture, blindfold, Bible

The Basics for Leaders

When David became king of Israel, God made a promise only he could make: that David's family would rule Israel forever.

Um . . . really? Go to Israel today and you won't find a king sitting on a throne. So did God actually keep this promise?

Absolutely—because *Jesus* was a part of David's family tree.

God knows the future. So if he says something will happen, you can be sure it will. God always keeps his promises, even if he doesn't keep them quite the way we expect him to do.

God promises to love us, but part of that love is when he disciplines us.

God promises we'll have a joyful life with him—but that doesn't mean we'll never flunk a test, lose a family member, or become seriously ill.

We *will* be joyful with God forever—in Heaven. And until we join him there, we can choose to be joyful now, no matter how hard our lives become.

As you experience this session with your kids, know that right now God is arranging things so he'll keep every awesome promise he's made to you!

HOWZITGOIN'

Time: about 5 minutes, depending on attendance
Supplies: pencils, prepared poster

Before kids arrive, draw a line on a poster. Place a 1 on the left end of the line, a 10 on the right, and a 5 in the middle. As kids arrive, ask them to pencil in their initials on the line.

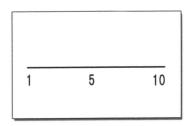

Say: **If this past week was so awful you wish you'd slept through it, place your initials by the 1. If it was a great week you wish you could repeat, put your initials by the 10. Place your initials anywhere on the line that shows how you feel about this past week—except exactly on the 5. That's because there's no such thing as a week that's exactly half good and half bad!**

After kids have signed in, give them 30 seconds each to explain why they placed their initials where they did. Be sure to include your own initials and explain your placement on the line. Kids will begin to express themselves more over time—and hearing their stories will help you adapt this lesson to make it relevant to your kids' lives.

KING/QUEEN FOR A DAY

Time: about 10 minutes
Supplies: newspaper, paper, markers, tape, safety scissors (several pairs)

Give children each a sheet of newspaper and sheet of paper. Place the markers, tape, and scissors where children can share them.

Tell children to create crowns for themselves—crowns they'll decorate any way they wish. Suggest they fashion a crown out of the newspaper and cut out decorations from the other paper. And yes, they'll wear the crowns.

Please do this activity yourself too. Your wearing a crown sends the signal that it's OK to look a bit silly for this activity!

After kids have completed their crowns, have them put on their crowns. Put on yours as well and gather everyone to sit in a circle. Say: **When we see someone wearing a crown, we know that person is royalty—often a king or queen. Let's take a moment and tell each other what's special about our crowns, what decorations we used—and why. My crown is special because . . .**

After you explain your crown, say: **Your turn now. Let's go around the circle and each show what's special about your crowns.**

After kids finish, thank them. Encourage them to keep their crowns on as you discuss together:

• *If you were really a king or queen, what's a rule you'd want to make?*

• *Who would you choose to give you advice on how to run the country? Why?*

• *If you were royalty, how important would it be to you that your kids and grandkids would get to be in charge after you die? Why?*

Say: **Today we're going to talk about someone who was really a king—a king who was promised that his family would rule the country forever. So did God keep his promise? We'll find out—but first let's practice being royalty ourselves!**

Awesome Promise Game

King/Queen Cruise
Time: about 10 minutes
Supplies: movable furniture, blindfold

Have the kids help move chairs or other furniture to create an obstacle course. Ask one child—still wearing his or her crown—to be the king/queen and go to the far end of the room. Ask the other kids to remove their crowns and station themselves around the room.

Explain that you'll blindfold the king/queen at the far end of the room. The king/queen's goal is to get through the course without running into anything—or anyone. That happens as everyone else acts as the king/queen's advisers. The children can call out directions for how to get through the course. They can decide for themselves whether they want to give good advice or bad advice to the blindfolded king/queen.

Have each child take a turn being the blindfolded king/queen and walking the course. After all kids have had a turn, have them sit in a circle and discuss:

• *When you were the king/queen, how did you know who was giving you good advice or bad advice?*

• *In real life how do you know whose advice to take?*

• *Tell about a time you took advice and it didn't end up being helpful.*

Say: **In a moment we'll talk about King David. When David was king he had to make a lot of decisions, and he had to trust people to give him good advice about what to do. Even kings can't know everything—they need advice.**

When David took wise advice—especially from God—his kingdom did well. When David or other kings who came after him took bad advice, bad things happened.

David discovered what we need to discover too: it's always a good idea to take God's advice! God knows the future and he loves us, so his advice is always good!

Let's find out more about King David!

Promise Kept BIBLE STORY

JESUS IS KING
Time: about 15 minutes
Supplies: Bible

To illustrate the passing of time in the Scriptures, kids will move with the scene changes. Ask children to first stand together in one corner of the room.

Say: **When God's people decided they wanted a king, God told them it was a bad idea. After all, *he* was their king. But they wanted a king they could see. One who would sit on a throne.**

God let them have a king, King Saul. And as God had predicted, it was a bad idea. So God helped them have a new king: David. Here's what David said.

Read aloud 2 Samuel 23:5.

Ask kids to move to the center of the room as a group. Say: **Years later, David's great-grandson was king of Israel. He said:**

Read aloud 2 Chronicles 13:4, 5.

Ask kids to move to the far side of the room as a group. Say: **Hundreds of years later, when Jesus was born, there was no great-great-great-great grandson of David ruling as the king in Israel. The country had been taken over by the Romans. So what happened?**

Many years before Jesus was born, the prophet Isaiah told God's people that God would send Jesus. And God even promised what family Jesus would be born into!

Read aloud Isaiah 9:6, 7 and then Matthew 1:1, 17.

Ask kids to sit down and, as a group, discuss:

- *In what ways did God keep his promises about Jesus?*
- *If Jesus is a king, where is his kingdom? If someone asked you to point out where it is, where would you point?*

Thank kids for sharing their thoughts. Say: **If someone asked me, "Where is Jesus the king?" I'd point to my heart. Jesus is king in my life. I hope he's the king in your life too!**

God knew the future when he made a promise to David, and God kept his awesome promise. Even if people don't honor God, Jesus is still king. And he's a king who will one day come back to earth. On that day everyone will know that Jesus is king.

We don't have to wait for that day though. We can honor Jesus as our king right now!

CLOSING PRAYER

PARTNER PRAYER
Time: about 5 minutes
Supplies: none

Ask kids to find partners. Say: **I'll lead us in prayer. I'll pause several times as I lead to give you the chance to share with your partner.**

Pray: **God, we know you're the same yesterday (in the past), today, and tomorrow (in the future). You're our king. Thank you for being with us in the past.**

Say: **Please take a moment and tell your partner something God has done for you in the past. For instance, God has let you have some good times with friends.** (pause as kids share)

Pray: **God, thank you for what you do for us now.**

Say: **Share something God is doing for you now. For instance, maybe he's helping you be a better friend.** (pause)

Pray: **Thank you for what you'll do for us in the future too.**

Say: **Tell your partner something you trust that God will do for you in the future. For instance, maybe you're trusting that God will let you grow up and learn to drive a car—a cool car!** (pause)

Pray: **Thank you again, God. You are a good king, and we love you. In Jesus' name, amen.**

EXTRA-TIME ACTIVITY—OPTION 1

WHADDYA KNOW?
Time: about 10 minutes
Supplies: none

Ask kids to form trios. If you have fewer than six kids, do this activity as a large group.

Explain the concept of a family tree, if your kids are unfamiliar. Then say: **Jesus could trace his family tree right back to King David. What do you** know about your family? Let's answer some questions—if we know the answers.** (Note: Be sensitive to any kids who have been adopted.)

- *Where are your grandparents from?*
- *What country is your family from?*
- *How did your parents meet?*
- *Are there physical characteristics that run in your family? For instance, is everyone short? Does everyone have brown eyes?*
- *Does your family celebrate any unusual holidays? If so, what are they?*
- *Do you have any special family photos or Bibles that have been passed down in your family?*
- *What's the story about your name? How was it chosen? Were you named after someone in your family?*

Say: **It's good to know our past, but God also knows our future! God promised David that his family would rule forever, and God kept his promise. God promised us that we can choose to be a part of his kingdom—and God will keep that promise too!**

EXTRA-TIME ACTIVITY—OPTION 2

HEADLINES

Time: about 10 minutes
Supplies: newspaper

Hold up a section of the newspaper. Read a few headlines about recent fires, car wrecks, or other disasters. Say: **Newspapers are good for telling us about bad things that have happened. But what if you had a newspaper that told you about bad things that were *going to* happen—and when? You'd know not to be in a building that was going to catch fire or not to be in a car that was going to crash.**

Ask kids to find partners and discuss:

- *If you could know about the bad things that are going to happen next week, would you want to know? Why or why not?*

- *Do you think God makes your future turn out a certain way?*
- *What good thing do you hope you get to do in the future?*

EXTRA-TIME ACTIVITY—OPTION 3

INQUIRING MINDS WANT TO KNOW

Time: about 5 minutes
Supplies: none

Gather kids in a circle. Ask: **How do you feel when you think about your future? Do you feel scared, happy, or something else?**

God's Promise
of a Savior

The Point: God sent Jesus for us.
Scripture Connect: Isaiah 9:6, 7; Luke 1:67-75

Supplies for all Session 5 activities options: pencils, prepared poster, Bible, prepared index cards, skein of yarn (or ball of twine)

The Basics for Leaders

Hundreds of years before Jesus arrived in Bethlehem, God (through a prophet) made the awesome promise: when the time was right, a Savior was coming.

God even gave his people some hints so they wouldn't miss Jesus when he showed up. He'd be born in Bethlehem. He'd be from a humble background. He'd grow up to do amazing things. Still, most people didn't connect the dots. They looked right at Jesus and didn't see him for who he was: the Savior.

And that's still the case. People look at Jesus and see a great leader. A skilled teacher. A good man.

And they're right . . . sort of. Jesus is all that—and more.

As you experience this session with your kids, help them see Jesus for who he really is: the Savior. *Their* Savior. And *your* Savior too.

OPENING ACTIVITY—OPTION 1

HOWZITGOIN'

Time: about 5 minutes, depending on attendance
Supplies: pencils, prepared poster

Before kids arrive, draw a line on a poster. Place a 1 on the left end of the line, a 10 on the right, and a 5 in the middle. As kids arrive, ask them to pencil in their initials on the line.

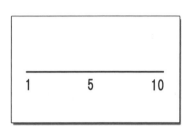

Say: **If this past week was so awful you wish you'd slept through it, place your initials by the 1. If it was a great week you wish you could repeat, put your initials by the 10. Place your initials anywhere on the line that shows how you feel about this past week—except exactly on the 5. That's because there's no such thing as a week that's exactly half good and half bad!**

After kids have signed in, give them 30 seconds each to explain why they placed their initials where they did. Be sure to include your own initials and explain your placement on the line. Kids will begin to express themselves more over time—and hearing their stories will help you adapt this lesson to make it relevant to your kids' lives.

OPENING ACTIVITY—OPTION 2

SUPERHERO

Time: about 10 minutes
Supplies: none

Have children pair up. Say: **Congratulations! You're all about to become superheroes! Costume, cape, cool hideout, the whole thing. But first you need a superhero name and a superpower. If I could have one superpower, I'd want . . .**

Briefly share what superpower you'd like. Model the sort of answer you'd like from the kids. Then say: **Your turn now. Talk with your partner about this:**

- *What superpower would you like to have?*
- *And what superhero name would you pick?*

Allow kids time to talk. Then have kids report their powers and names to the larger group.

Say: **The point of being a superhero is to save people from danger. Sometimes people get in tough spots where they need to be saved. For instance, if you can't swim and you end up in deep water, you need to be saved. Or maybe if you are confused about a subject in school, you need help.**

- *Who has a story about a time you needed to be saved?*

Allow time for stories. Thank kids for sharing.

Say: **In at least one way, we all need to be saved. And good news: God promised something about that. We'll find out more about that promise, but first let's rescue someone!**

Awesome Promise Game

Rescue Rope
Time: about 10 minutes
Supplies: none

Say: **Uh-oh. One of your friends fell off a cliff and is clinging to a branch. Your friend will fall unless you throw down a rope. Who has a rope?**

Pause while kids realize no one has a rope. Explain that together your kids will have to make a rope out of what they have with them. Ask kids to see how long a rope they could create by placing end to end on the floor their shoelaces, belts, sweaters, and other objects they have with them.

When kids have finished creating their rope, have them retrieve their belongings and put themselves back together as you discuss:

• *Would you rather be a person helping someone, or a person being helped? Why?*

• *What would you say if your friend clinging to the branch wouldn't trust you or the rope—and wouldn't grab hold?*

Say: **Sometimes it's hard to admit we need help. We like to take care of ourselves, to be strong. But we all need help in at least one way: we need God's help with our sins. We've all done things we shouldn't have done, said things we shouldn't have said. We haven't always lived in ways that pleased God, so we all need God's forgiveness. Let's find out how one of God's promises is part of the story of forgiveness.**

Promise Kept BIBLE STORY

STEREO BIBLE ACTING

Time: about 15 minutes
Supplies: Bible, prepared index cards

Before the session, write each of these terms from Isaiah 9:6, 7 on a separate index card: "Wonderful Counselor," "Mighty God," "Everlasting Father," "Prince of Peace." Also write on index cards these two phrases from Luke 1:67-75: "mighty Savior," "saved from our enemies and from all who hate us."

Form kids into two groups and have the groups stand on different sides of the room. Explain that in a few minutes, you'll read two passages from the Bible. The first group will strike poses to show what was special about Jesus, according to the names he was given in Isaiah 9:6, 7. Then the second group will strike poses that reflect what Jesus came to do and be, according to Luke 1:67-75.

Give each group their index cards and a couple of minutes to discuss how they will strike a pose to convey these meanings. You should help both groups with ideas as they rehearse.

Now read the passages aloud, pausing at the mention of each description on the cards, so groups can strike poses that reflect those descriptions.

Afterwards, have both groups join you in the middle of the room, sit in a circle, and discuss:

- *In what ways do you think Jesus did—or didn't—do all the things God said he'd do?*
- *Isaiah promised that Jesus would come for people, and Jesus showed up. But he showed up 2,000 years ago. Do you think he came for us in this room too? If so, where is he?*
- *Jesus is a "mighty Savior." One reason God sent Jesus was so we could serve God without being afraid* (see Luke 1:74). *In what ways can you serve God?*

Say: **When God promised to send Jesus, God knew that Jesus would die on a cross. But Jesus came anyway—because he loves us that much. I'm so glad that Jesus came . . . and rose from the dead . . . and that through Jesus we can have our sins forgiven! Jesus came to save people who lived thousands of years ago, and he can save us today too!**

CLOSING PRAYER

BECAUSE/I WILL PRAYER
Time: about 5 minutes
Supplies: none

Ask kids to join you in a circle. Say: **Sometimes people use "Because/I will" statements. For instance, I might say, "Because I'm tired, I will go to bed" or "Because I'm hungry, I will eat."**

Let's do a "Because/I will" prayer. I'll say a "because" statement, and you fill in the "I will" part. For instance, "Because God sent Jesus . . . I will be saved." Say your "I will" statements out loud, and it's OK if you all say them at the same time. They're our prayers. God is here with us, listening.

Say each of the following and pause for the kids to fill in the rest.

Because God loves us . . . (pause)

Because God keeps his awesome promises . . . (pause)

Because God wants us to be close to him . . . (pause)
Because God sent Jesus . . . (pause)

Finish your prayer with: **God, we thank you for your great love and for keeping your promise to send Jesus. In Jesus' name, amen.**

EXTRA-TIME ACTIVITY—OPTION 1

DON'T TRY THIS ALONE
Time: about 10 minutes
Supplies: none

Ask kids to partner up with someone about their own size. Ask pairs to move so there's room between them.

Say: **Get toe-to-toe with your partner and hold your partner's hands. Now both of you lean back slowly, pretending to sit in a chair. See how long you can sit on your "not there chair."**

Allow kids several tries to succeed at this task, and then have pairs sit on the floor back-to-back, feet flat on the floor. Have partners link elbows behind themselves and push against each other to stand up together. Then have them stay linked and slowly sit down as they push against each other.

This is tough, so applaud their efforts! As a group, discuss:

• *How well could you have done either of those tasks without a partner to help you?*

• *You relied on your partner to "save" you by helping you. In what ways do you count on other partners in life to help you?* (Kids will need help identifying who counts as a partner.)

• *In what ways do others count on you for your help?*

• *In what ways does Jesus help or save you?*

EXTRA-TIME ACTIVITY—OPTION 2

WONDER WEB

Time: about 10 minutes
Supplies: skein of yarn (or ball of twine)

Form kids into a circle and have kids take two steps back so there are 2 to 3 feet between them. Explain: **I'm so glad God kept his promise to send a Savior! I know that God keeps his promises, but I don't know everything about God. Sometimes I have questions. I'll hold one end of the yarn and toss the rest of it to someone in the circle but who isn't right next to me. As I do, I'll say something that I wonder about. For instance, I might say, "I wonder if there will be animals in Heaven" or "I wonder why God made mosquitoes."**

Explain that the person you toss the yarn to will repeat the process. Everyone must receive the yarn once before it's tossed twice to anyone. Your goal as a group: get the yarn to everyone at least twice before you run out of things to say.

Say: **Here we go. As we hear what we wonder about God or about God's promises, we'll create a giant Wonder Web!**

Toss around the yarn. Don't be in a rush; give kids time to think.

After kids share, thank them for sharing their "wonderings." (And make a note of the issues they raised. Those will make great topics for future meetings!)

EXTRA-TIME ACTIVITY—OPTION 3

INQUIRING MINDS WANT TO KNOW

Time: about 5 minutes
Supplies: none

Gather kids in a circle. Ask: *If God sent Jesus and wants us to believe in Jesus, why doesn't Jesus just appear to everyone in person so everyone will believe in him?*

God's Promise
to Zechariah
and Elizabeth

The Point: God does for us what he promises.
Scripture Connect: Luke 1:5-20, 57-64

Supplies for all Session 6 activities options: pencils, prepared poster, wastebasket, coins (3 per child), paper, markers, Bible

The Basics for Leaders

God promised that Zechariah and Elizabeth would have a baby—and what a baby! Their son would grow up to be part of the greatest story ever. He'd point straight at the Savior, letting everyone know that God had shown up in person.

But there was a problem: Elizabeth couldn't have children. That is, without God's power she couldn't have children.

Zechariah and Elizabeth knew all about God. Zechariah was a priest, and Elizabeth came from a long line of priests. They'd grown up learning about God and had given their lives to serving God. They were rock solid, but somewhere along the line they'd missed an important lesson. It's the lesson you'll share with your kids today.

It doesn't matter if God's awesome promises seem impossible. God's good at impossible. God does impossible with one hand tied behind his back!

As you experience this session with your kids, celebrate with them the truth that God does for us what he promises—always.

OPENING ACTIVITY—OPTION 1

HOWZITGOIN'

Time: about 5 minutes, depending on attendance
Supplies: pencils, prepared poster

Before kids arrive, draw a line on a poster. Place a 1 on the left end of the line, a 10 on the right, and a 5 in the middle. As kids arrive, ask them to pencil in their initials on the line.

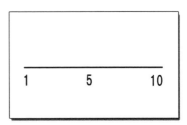

Say: **If this past week was so awful you wish you'd slept through it, place your initials by the 1. If it was a great week you wish you could repeat, put your initials by the 10. Place your initials anywhere on the line that shows how you feel about this past week—except exactly on the 5. That's because there's no such thing as a week that's exactly half good and half bad!**

After kids have signed in, give them 30 seconds each to explain why they placed their initials where they did. Be sure to include your own initials and explain your placement on the line. Kids will begin to express themselves more over time—and hearing their stories will help you adapt this lesson to make it relevant to your kids' lives.

OPENING ACTIVITY—OPTION 2

CALL IT COIN TOSS

Time: about 10 minutes
Supplies: wastebasket, coins (3 per child)

Place a wastebasket on the floor. Have kids form a circle, shoulder to shoulder, around it. Give each child three coins.

Ask: **How many of you predict (that is, say ahead of time) that you can toss your three coins into the basket without a miss?**

Have them predict, then toss, and then retrieve their coins. Re-form the circle, having kids turn so they're facing away from the wastebasket. Then each person should take one step. Repeat the "predict, toss, and retrieve" process, having kids toss their coins *over* their shoulders. Do the activity again from two steps away, and then five. Kids' ability to predict accurately will fade the farther they get from the wastebasket.

Gather coins and have kids sit together. Discuss:

• *What happened to your predictions as we played the game? Why?*

• *What made it easy or hard to make predictions that were on target?*

Say: **We all make predictions about what we think will happen. And we also make promises about what we are *sure* will happen. Maybe you've promised a parent you'll clean your room or turn in a homework assignment on time. We're sure we'll come through, but sometimes we don't.**

I'll bet we've all made a promise that we didn't keep. For me it was . . .

Briefly share a promise you made that you didn't keep. You'll model the sort of response you hope to hear from kids. Then say:

• *Now it's your turn. Tell about a promise you didn't keep. What was the promise, and why didn't you keep it?*

After kids share, thank them and say: **Today we'll talk about an awesome promise that God made to a married couple. And the promise was hard to believe. But first, let's see what sort of predictions and promises you have about yourself!**

Awesome Promise Game

Wonder Words
Time: about 10 minutes
Supplies: paper, markers

Give each child a sheet of paper and a marker. Say: **Time to make some predictions and promises. Think about what you'll be doing in a week. Write some words or draw pictures of what you think you'll be doing in a week. Write or draw small—I'll ask you to add more in a minute.**

Assure kids that spelling isn't important in this activity. Give them several minutes to write or draw.

Say: **Now think about five years from now. How old will that make you?** (pause to let kids do the math) **Write or draw what you think you'll be doing then.**

Pause for several minutes as kids write or draw.

Then say: **Now think about when you'll be a grown-up. Write or draw what you think you'll be doing then.**

Pause for several minutes as kids write or draw.

Ask kids to take turns showing what they wrote or drew. If you have lots of kids, group them into pairs or trios and let them show their papers in those smaller groups. The goal is for everyone to have the chance to talk.

Then ask the whole group to gather in a circle and discuss:

- *How sure are you that what you think you'll be doing in a week will really happen? Why?*

- *How sure are you of your predictions for five years from now? for your grown-up years? Why?*

- *If I promised you that something on your sheet of paper would happen, how sure would you be that it would happen?*

Say: **I don't know your future. I can't know it. But God knows. And when God promises something will happen for you in the future, you can count on it. A couple named Zechariah and Elizabeth learned that God does for us what he promises. Let's hear their story now.**

(Note: Keep the kids' papers for the Wonder Words Prayer activity.)

Promise Kept BIBLE STORY

2 KIDS = 1 ACTOR

Time: about 15 minutes
Supplies: Bible

(Note: Depending on your group, you may want to read the Scripture aloud once and then have your volunteer actors perform during a second read.)

Ask for two volunteers of the same sex and approximately the same size. Have them stand in the front of the room, facing the rest of the kids, one behind the other. The child in the rear will extend his arms under the front person's arms, and the front person will place his arms behind the other's back.

As they act out the story you read, the front person will provide voices and facial expressions; the person in the back will provide hand movements.

Ask your "actor" to act out the actions of all the characters as you read aloud Luke 1:5-20, 57-64.

Lead the rest of the kids in applauding your volunteers' efforts and then, as a group, discuss:

• **God made Zechariah unable to speak. Do you think that was a fair punishment for doubting that God would keep a promise?**

• **If God punished you for doubting him, how much trouble would you be in? Why?**

• **When you hear "God does for us what he promises," how do you feel?**

• **What's a promise that you're afraid God won't keep?**

Say: **When Zechariah's voice was returned, the first thing he did was praise God. Let's use our voices to praise God through our prayers.**

CLOSING PRAYER

WONDER WORDS PRAYER

Time: about 5 minutes
Supplies: Bible, kids' papers from the Wonder Words activity

Ask kids to stand and to pick up their Wonder Words papers. Place the Bible on a chair or stool.

Say: **Some kids are scared of the future. They worry that a day will come when they don't have any friends or their families won't have any money. I don't know what will come in my life or yours, but I do know this: God promises to be with us no matter what. I don't have to be afraid of what's coming—and you don't have to be afraid either.**

Pray: **God, thank you for loving us. We trust you with our lives and our futures. We know you'll do for us what you've promised.**

Then say to the kids: **If you'd like to trust your future to God, place your Wonder Words paper on the Bible. Then come back and we'll thank God for being with us.**

After those kids who want to place their papers on the Bible do so, invite them to pray out loud, thanking and praising God.

Close by praying: **Thank you for always being true to your Word, God. In Jesus' name, amen.**

EXTRA-TIME ACTIVITY—OPTION 1

HEADS OR TAILS
Time: about 10 minutes
Supplies: coins (3 per child)

Give each child three coins. Form kids into trios. Ask children to, in their trios, each flip a coin at the same time (tossing the coins in the air and catching them will work for kids who can't flip coins). After they flip coins they will compare their coins. If two of the coins are the same (heads or tails) and one coin is different, whoever has the different coin will take the other two pennies. In this game, being unusual actually pays!

Continue to play. The game in each trio ends when one child runs out of coins. Then the two kids with coins count how many coins they have, and the one with the most is crowned Trio Coin King (or Queen).

After playing for a few minutes, collect the pennies and have kids discuss:
- **When you started this game, did you expect to win? Why?**

- *How do you feel about starting things when you don't know how they'll turn out?*
- *If you could know for sure how one thing in your life is going to turn out, what would you choose to know about? Why did you choose that?*

Say: **Zechariah and Elizabeth didn't know what their future would hold. Then they were given a promise by God. We can trust all of God's promises. God always does for us what he promises to do.**

EXTRA-TIME ACTIVITY—OPTION 2

BLESSINGS
Time: about 10 minutes
Supplies: none

Ask children to separate around the room and sit quietly on the floor. Say: **I don't know what's coming in your future, but I know God has given you gifts and talents he'll use as you move into your future.**

Move from child to child. When you reach each child, take the child's hand (or place your hand on his or her shoulder), look into the child's eyes, and briefly bless the child. Using the child's name, say something like: (Child's name), **God loves you very much and has given you the gift of a great sense of humor** (or whatever attribute you wish to affirm). **I know God will use you and your gift in the future if you give your future to him.**

EXTRA-TIME ACTIVITY—OPTION 3

INQUIRING MINDS WANT TO KNOW
Time: about 5 minutes
Supplies: none

Gather kids in a circle. Ask: ***God always does what he promises to do. What promise of God do you wish he wouldn't keep—if any?***

Jesus' Promise
to a Woman
in Pain

The Point: We can count on Jesus' power.
Scripture Connect: Luke 13:10-13

Supplies for all Session 7 activities options: pencils, prepared poster, several 2-page newspaper spreads, canned foods (1 per child), Bible, watch with a second hand, blank label stickers (1 per child), markers

The Basics for Leaders

Jesus' awesome promise to the woman who had been doubled over for eighteen years: she'd be healed. Even better, she'd be healed immediately. Jesus kept his promise and, with a touch, gave the woman back her ability to stand upright.

Two things to notice:

1. The woman didn't ask Jesus for his help. She was just in the synagogue, coming to worship, when Jesus saw her. He called her over to where he was teaching and gave her back the gift of her health.

2. Her response was as immediate as her healing: she praised God!

As you share this session with your kids, be open to experiencing what the woman experienced. Be open to God's reaching into your life and offering you healing in some way. And be open to reacting the same way the woman did—by praising God.

OPENING ACTIVITY—OPTION 1

HOWZITGOIN'
Time: about 5 minutes, depending on attendance
Supplies: pencils, prepared poster

Before kids arrive, draw a line on a poster. Place a 1 on the left end of the line, a 10 on the right, and a 5 in the middle. As kids arrive, ask them to pencil in their initials on the line.

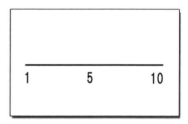

Say: **If this past week was so awful you wish you'd slept through it, place your initials by the 1. If it was a great week you wish you could repeat, put your initials by the 10. Place your initials anywhere on the line that shows how you feel about this past week—except exactly on the 5. That's because there's no such thing as a week that's exactly half good and half bad!**

After kids have signed in, give them 30 seconds each to explain why they placed their initials where they did. Be sure to include your own initials and explain your placement on the line. Kids will begin to express themselves more over time—and hearing their stories will help you adapt this lesson to make it relevant to your kids' lives.

OPENING ACTIVITY—OPTION 2

SEATED SUMO WRESTLING
Time: about 10 minutes
Supplies: several 2-page newspaper spreads

Place a newspaper spread on the floor—preferably on a carpeted area.

Pair up kids with kids of about the same size. Have the first pair sit on the newspaper spread, facing each other. Have the kids in the pair lean forward, grasping each other's forearms.

Explain: **The goal of the game is to get your opponent to tip off the newspaper spread—but each contestant must remain seated the entire time. And no head butts!**

Allow up to 30 seconds for each match. Declare a winner if a child is able to force his or her partner to tip over, moving off the spread. If you have lots of kids, have several pairs compete at once.

When every pair has had a chance to try this, clear away the newspapers. Then gather kids together in a circle on the floor and discuss:

- *What made this activity tough?*
- *What plan would you use to win if you were to play this again?*

Say: **In this activity it wasn't just your size that mattered. Balance and surprise helped you win too. Sometimes what makes us powerful isn't how big we are but is something else.**

Can you think of a time when you saw someone small be powerful? Maybe it was a teacher who wasn't big, but she could make everyone quiet down with just a look. One time I saw someone small be powerful was when . . .

Briefly tell about a time you saw someone small be powerful. Then say: **Your turn now.**

Let kids share stories. Then thank them and say: **Today we'll talk about someone who didn't look all that big or strong. He didn't have an army. He wasn't nine feet tall. He didn't carry a weapon. But he was powerful—really powerful. More powerful than anyone else!**

But first, let's show how powerful our noses are!

Awesome Promise Game

Nose Bowling

Time: about 10 minutes
Supplies: canned foods (1 per child)

Give each child a can of food. (Note: Don't use empty cans. Sharp edges of opened cans are a bad combination with noses!) In an open area have kids line up against one wall, get on their hands and knees, and place their cans on the floor in front of them.

Explain that the goal of the game is to push their cans to the finish line (the far wall or any other line you establish) using only their noses. Once kids are in position, count down to "Go!" and launch them. (Note: Adapt for girls wearing skirts.)

Have kids return their cans to the starting line using their pinkies. Want to play additional rounds? Use tops of heads . . . or ears . . . or chins.

Collect the cans and have kids sit. As a group, discuss:

• **Which way of powering up your can did you like most? least? Why?**

• **What gets you powered up? When do you feel the strongest?**

• **What are some ways that people show they're powerful?**

Say: **Jesus showed his power in lots of ways. Let's meet a woman who discovered just how powerful Jesus was!**

Promise Kept BIBLE STORY

STRAIGHTEN UP
Time: about 15 minutes
Supplies: Bible

Ask children to stand in a circle and then to see if they can bend at the waist and touch their toes. Have them try twice to limber up; then ask them to bend over and touch their toes—and keep touching their toes as you read. Read aloud Luke 13:10-13.

Ask kids to slowly straighten back up and then to sit with you in a circle. As a group, discuss:

• **What was it like being bent over? How would your life change if you were stuck in that position?**

• **How has Jesus helped heal you—or has that ever happened?**

• **If you could choose one person for Jesus to heal, who would it be? Why?**

Say: **The woman Jesus healed was happy about being healed. She praised God for Jesus' awesome promise to her—that her sickness had left her. And I'll bet she sent any of her friends who were in pain to see Jesus too! Let's go to Jesus now to tell him about people we know who are in pain—and ask that he heal them.**

CLOSING PRAYER

PAINFUL PRAYER

Time: about 5 minutes
Supplies: none

Ask kids to create space between each other and to lie on their backs on the floor.

Say: **Imagine that you can't move, that you're trapped in the position you're in.** (pause) **Now imagine that you *can* move, but every move hurts terribly.** (pause) **There are many people in both those situations—they're paralyzed or injured. Or like the woman Jesus healed, they're bent and weak.**

Please think of someone you know who needs to be healed. Perhaps it's someone who has been injured or has a disease. Or whose body is fine, but the person is in another sort of pain. Perhaps the person's family member has died, or the person lost a job or is hurting (or sad) for some other reason.

Now silently pray for that person. Ask Jesus to please heal that person, if he will. I'll close the prayer in a minute.

After 60 seconds, pray: **God, thank you that you know the people we've been telling you about. You know everything. Thank you that you have the power to bring those people comfort and healing. We ask you to help the people we've prayed for. And if you want to use us to bring them comfort, help us to do that. In Jesus' name, amen.**

THUMB WAR

Time: about 10 minutes
Supplies: watch with a second hand

Have kids pair up. Say: **Time to see who's most powerful . . . by going to war! Thumb war!**

Explain the rules: **Each pair sits facing each other and grasps the fingers of their right hands, leaving their thumbs sticking up. The object of the game is to pin an opponent's thumb under your thumb. To do this you can't use anything other than your thumb. A player will be considered "pinned" if he can't free his thumb in three seconds.**

Announce that you'll play three rounds, and each round can't last longer than 60 seconds. If neither player in a pair is pinned in that time, that round will be considered a tie.

Begin each round with a chant that lets players get ready: "One, two, three, four. I will win this thumb war."

After playing three rounds, have opponents shake hands (no pinning thumbs!) and sit next to each other in a circle on the floor with you. As a group, discuss:

• *Those of you who won your thumb wars, how does it feel to show your power?*

• *Those of you who were "thumbhow" defeated, how does it feel not to win a power struggle like this?*

• *Tell about a time you either won or lost a contest. What was it, and how did it feel?*

• *What kind of good things can you choose to do when you have power?*

EXTRA-TIME ACTIVITY—OPTION 2

POWERED BY GOD

Time: about 10 minutes
Supplies: blank label stickers (1 per child), markers

Give each child a sticker and a marker. Say: **I'd like you to make a sticker to wear. On it please write, "Powered by God." How you write it—how you design your sticker—is up to you. But please put that message on the sticker.**

AGE-ALERT TIPS

You or **older children** will need to write the words for **younger children.**

Give kids several minutes to design and put on their stickers. Then as a group, discuss:

▪ *How can you tell whether someone is powered by God or powered by something else?*

▪ *In what ways are our stickers true? In what ways aren't they true?*

▪ *If you stay powered by God, what might God do with you?*

Say: **We can choose to follow Jesus and be powered by God, or try to run our own lives without God. I want to be powered by God, because I know we can count on his power!**

EXTRA-TIME ACTIVITY—OPTION 3

INQUIRING MINDS WANT TO KNOW

Time: about 5 minutes
Supplies: none

Gather kids in a circle. Ask: *If Jesus is powerful and loving and we can count on Jesus' power, why doesn't he heal everyone?*

Jesus' Promise
to Rise from
the Dead

The Point: Jesus is God.
Scripture Connect: Luke 9:21-23; Matthew 28:1-7

Supplies for all Session 8 activities options: pencils, prepared poster, paper, markers, blanket (or large towel), watch with a second hand, paper clips (and other options; see instructions), flour (or white play sand, if kids have gluten allergies), ¼ cup scoop, colored paper plates (1 per child), large work table, newspaper or drop cloth (optional), Bible, newspaper obituaries

The Basics for Leaders

Jesus' promise: that after three days in a grave, he'd rise to life again.

If that's not true, Jesus is just another teacher (if not a liar!) whose words end up on a poster or in a book. But if it *is* true? Then it changes . . . well, everything.

It changes how you live. Why you live. What you can expect after you quit living (at least here on earth) . . .

So what do you believe? Really believe? Did Jesus keep this awesome promise? You see, Jesus not only promised that he would rise from the dead; he promised that if you love and follow him, you'll do the same thing. And if there was power for *him* to do it, there's power for you too.

As you experience this session, you're helping your kids explore the single most important truth in their Christian faith.

OPENING ACTIVITY—OPTION 1

HOWZITGOIN'

Time: about 5 minutes, depending on attendance
Supplies: pencils, prepared poster

Before kids arrive, draw a line on a poster. Place a 1 on the left end of the line, a 10 on the right, and a 5 in the middle. As kids arrive, ask them to pencil in their initials on the line.

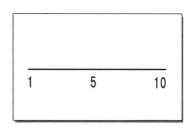

Say: **If this past week was so awful you wish you'd slept through it, place your initials by the 1. If it was a great** week you wish you could repeat, put your initials by the 10. Place your initials anywhere on the line that shows how you feel about this past week—except exactly on the 5. That's because there's no such thing as a week that's exactly half good and half bad!

After kids have signed in, give them 30 seconds each to explain why they placed their initials where they did. Be sure to include your own initials and explain your placement on the line. Kids will begin to express themselves more over time—and hearing their stories will help you adapt this lesson to make it relevant to your kids' lives.

OPENING ACTIVITY—OPTION 2

SHADOW SKETCHES

Time: about 10 minutes
Supplies: paper, markers

Let children pair up. Give each child a sheet of paper and marker.

Say: **Did you ever see an artist create a silhouette? They stand people sideways and then sketch just the outline of their heads. They sometimes frame the silhouettes in a cardboard frame, kind of**

like a cheap painting. We're all about being cheap, so it's silhouette time!

Explain that each child will draw a silhouette of his or her partner. The child in each pair whose birthday is larger (the 25th is larger than the 3rd) will pose first. Kids should keep everyone, including their partners, from seeing their work. When finished, kids will fold their sheets of paper and give them to you. Stress that this is to be a serious effort—no silly or mean pictures!

Allow up to two minutes for each silhouette. Then collect the sheets of paper and shuffle them. Then open them and display each. See whether the group can identify the subject of each sketch. Then say: **Sometimes we have features that remind people of our parents or grandparents. For me it's . . .**

Briefly point out a feature of yours that is a family trait. Your hair color or height, for instance.

Say: **Your turn now. Maybe you know a feature because people point it out. Maybe you don't know your birth parents, and you'll have to guess. Either way works.**

▪ *What do you think is a feature that shows up in others in your family?*

▪ *If you could choose one feature or trait from a parent or even a great-great-great grandparent and have it show up, what would it be? For instance, maybe your grandmother is a good artist or your uncle is very rich. Why would you choose that feature or trait?*

▪ *Some people say "like father, like son." What do you think about that? Are people in families pretty much the same, or are they different?*

▪ *How are you like or different from your parents?*

Say: **Thanks for talking about your families. I know you better now—and I like that! Today we're going to talk about another father and son and how they're alike. But first, let's play a game I call Don't Fall into the Lava!**

Awesome Promise Game

Don't Fall into the Lava

Time: about 10 minutes

Supplies: blanket (or large towel), watch with a second hand, paper clips (and other options)

Select a blanket on which your kids can stand but will be crowded. If you have just a few kids, use a large towel. Before kids arrive, secretly do something to the blanket so one side is different from the other. For example, attach a couple of paper clips on the edge, sew on a colored thread, and add a small piece of tape. Add details that are small, but noticeable if you look.

Ask children to remove their shoes. Spread the blanket on the floor ("different" side down) and have kids stand on it. Explain that the kids are on an island. The floor around them is red-hot lava. Their challenge is to turn over the blanket and stand on the other side without anyone stepping off the blanket and into the lava in the process.

Time how long it takes. Allow them to try again to see if they can do it more quickly. Have them do it again while seated. Then gather everyone in a circle, sitting on or around the blanket. Discuss:

- *What made this activity easy or hard?*
- *Which side of the blanket was safer for not falling into the lava?*
- *Without looking down at the blanket, describe the differences between the two sides.*

After kids describe the differences they recall, have them investigate. Point out the paper clips, thread, tape, and any other details you planted and they missed.

Say: **Even though there are some differences, you can tell that both sides of the blanket are the same blanket. Two sides, one blanket. It's important to know that Jesus and God are one, sort of like two sides of the same blanket. Jesus told people that when they looked at him, they were looking at God (John 10:30; 14:7). That's because when Jesus was on earth, he was God with skin on. But the people were like us with the blanket—they didn't see all the details. We should remember that when we trust Jesus, we're trusting God. And Jesus didn't just *say* he was God; he proved it. Let's find out more.**

Promise Kept BIBLE STORY

FLOUR POWER

Time: about 15 minutes

Supplies: flour (or white play sand, if kids have gluten allergies), ¼ cup scoop, colored paper plates (1 per child), large work table, newspapers or drop cloth (optional), Bible

(Note: If you're concerned about the mess, spread newspapers or a drop cloth on the floor.) Give each child a plate at a large work table. Place ¼ cup of flour on each plate. Demonstrate how kids can use a finger to trace a picture on the plate. As the flour moves, the color of the plate will be visible.

Ask children to listen to the Bible reading and to "sketch" on their plates the scene of Jesus' crucifixion or the tomb where he was buried. Read aloud the sad parts of today's Scripture: Luke 9:22 and Matthew 28:1.

After kids have sketched, have them carefully move around to examine each others' art. Then, as a group, discuss:

• How do you think Jesus' friends and family felt when he was nailed to a cross?

• If you'd been one of Jesus' followers, how would you have felt to know he'd been buried in a tomb?

• How do you feel now when you think about all the pain Jesus must have felt?

Ask children to gently shake their own plates to erase their artwork.

Say: **The good news is that, because Jesus is God, he rose from the dead! We don't have to feel sad about what happened, because something wonderful came from it.**

Read aloud Matthew 28:2-7 and ask kids to sketch how they feel knowing that Jesus is alive. When they finish, let them look at each others' art again.

Say: **Jesus promised to rise from the dead, and he did it. I'm glad! Let's thank Jesus for who he is and for all he's done.**

CLOSING PRAYER

BLANKET PRAYER

Time: about 5 minutes
Supplies: blanket

Ask kids to join you in holding the blanket by its edges. Be sure each child is holding part of the blanket, and that the blanket is held at waist height. Say: **Let's use this blanket to thank Jesus for what he's done for us.**

Encourage kids to offer sentence prayers, thanking Jesus for living for us. You begin.

Then have kids lower the blanket to just six inches from the floor. Say: **While it's here close to the ground, please join me in thanking Jesus for dying for us.**

Encourage kids to offer sentence prayers. You begin.

When they've finished, ask them to raise the blanket to shoulder height. Encourage kids to offer sentence prayers, thanking Jesus for rising from the dead. You start.

When they've finished, raise the blanket high overhead. Encourage kids to thank Jesus for his awesome promise to come back someday. You begin. When they've finished, lower the blanket as you pray, **In Jesus' name, amen.**

EXTRA-TIME ACTIVITY—OPTION 1

DRUM BEAT

Time: about 10 minutes
Supplies: none

Ask kids to circle up and sit on the floor. Using your hands on the floor, establish the beat of "We will, we will rock you," a refrain often heard in sports arenas and on classic rock stations.

You'll be chanting "Jesus, Jesus is God." Ask kids to call out words that describe Jesus at the appropriate time in the rhythm. For instance, after chanting "Jesus, Jesus is God," someone might shout out "Strong!" or "Faithful!"

Practice the beat until it becomes almost automatic for your kids, and then see how long you can keep it going with descriptions of Jesus. Then discuss:

- **If Jesus is all those things—if he's God—why do you think he cares about people like us?**
- **What difference does knowing Jesus make in how you act?**

EXTRA-TIME ACTIVITY—OPTION 2

OBITS

Time: about 10 minutes
Supplies: newspaper obituaries

Briefly explain what an obituary is, and then read several from the newspaper. As a group, pray for the families of those who have died.

Say: **When you love and follow Jesus, you have the promise that dying is just a bad day. The next thing you know, you're with him— forever—in Heaven. Because Jesus is God and rose from the dead, through his power we'll rise too. We don't need to be afraid of dying. Let's be thankful for the hope we have in Jesus!**

EXTRA-TIME ACTIVITY—OPTION 3

INQUIRING MINDS WANT TO KNOW

Time: about 5 minutes
Supplies: none

Gather kids in a circle. Ask: ***Jesus promised that we'd rise from the dead too. Does the idea of rising from the dead make you happy, scared, or something else? Why?***

God's Promise
to See and
Love Us

The Point: God knows what's happening to us—and cares.
Scripture Connect: Psalm 139:1, 2; Matthew 10:29-31

Supplies for all Session 9 activities options: pencils, prepared poster, index cards (2 per child), markers, masking tape, paper plates (1 per child), safety scissors (1 pair per child), lamp (or flashlight), Bible, large bowl of water, paper towels

The Basics for Leaders

Here's God's awesome promise to you: he sees you. He knows what's happening in your life—and he cares.

There are times when that promise might be hard to believe. Like when you're in pain. Or when divorce or illness or a flunked test drags you down. Does God know that you're struggling? If so, why doesn't he do something about it? How can someone tell you he cares when he lets the fever get higher, or your bank account get lower?

The truth is, those who were listening when Jesus told them about God's care were in the same spot you're in. Their lives weren't perfect. Some were sick. Some were poor. Yet Jesus told them God saw them—and cared.

That was true for them, and it's true for you. Jesus never said we'd get lives free from pain and suffering. What he promised is that we're loved and that he'll walk through the tough times with us.

As you experience this session with your kids, be looking for how God is working in your life—even in the tender spots.

OPENING ACTIVITY—OPTION 1

HOWZITGOIN'

Time: about 5 minutes, depending on attendance
Supplies: pencils, prepared poster

Before kids arrive, draw a line on a poster. Place a 1 on the left end of the line, a 10 on the right, and a 5 in the middle. As kids arrive, ask them to pencil in their initials on the line.

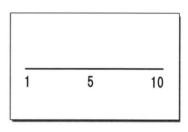

Say: **If this past week was so awful you wish you'd slept through it, place your initials by the 1. If it was a great week you wish you could repeat, put your initials by the 10. Place your initials anywhere on the line that shows how you feel about this past week—except exactly on the 5. That's because there's no such thing as a week that's exactly half good and half bad!**

After kids have signed in, give them 30 seconds each to explain why they placed their initials where they did. Be sure to include your own initials and explain your placement on the line. Kids will begin to express themselves more over time—and hearing their stories will help you adapt this lesson to make it relevant to your kids' lives.

OPENING ACTIVITY—OPTION 2

WHO AM I?

Time: about 10 minutes
Supplies: index cards (2 per child), markers, masking tape

Give each child two index cards and a marker. Say: **Choose two famous characters and write their names, one name on each of your cards. Don't let anyone see what you're writing! The famous characters** can be real people from long ago or people who are alive today . . . or can even be cartoon or movie characters—but they should be characters that we all know. For instance, you might write "the president" or "Mickey Mouse." Also put your own initials on your cards.

AGE-ALERT TIPS
Younger children may need your help, both thinking of famous characters and writing the names.

Collect completed cards. Tape a card on each child's back, making sure that no child gets a card he or she has written (hold the extra cards for another round). Explain that the goal is to guess what name is on your back by asking questions to which the group will answer yes or no.

Say: **Don't give any other hints. Let's see if everyone can guess his or her name in a few seconds!**

Play two rounds, replacing the guessed cards with the second set of cards. Then have the group discuss:

- *How did it feel not to know who you were?*
- *What helped you figure out who you were? What got in your way?*
- *What would have happened if you'd been given the name of someone you didn't know at all?*

Say: **God doesn't have the problem of not knowing people. God promises that he'll see us, know us, and care about us. That means the God who created the universe knows what you had for lunch yesterday! And what you're thinking right now. He knows you—and he loves you. When God says it, it's a promise!**

We'll talk more about that promise, but first let's play a game I call Who Knew Turn Around.

Awesome Promise Game

Who Knew Turn Around
Time: about 10 minutes
Supplies: none

Ask kids to sit in a circle on the floor. Join them. Say: **Even if some of us have known each other for a long time, there are things we don't know. For example, I . . .**

Share something appropriate that kids won't know about you. For instance, maybe you broke your leg when you were young, or you're able to yodel.

If a child already knew the fact you shared about yourself, turn around and face away from the circle. Each child will take a turn sharing something that, supposedly, nobody in the circle already knows. If someone *does* know the fact that's shared, the child who shared it will turn around and face away from the circle. Everyone will continue to listen and play, but only those who tell completely surprising facts will continue to sit facing toward the center of the circle.

Go around your circle twice. If a child who had to turn away from the circle the first time tells a fact nobody knows the second time, he or she can again face toward the center of the circle.

After you've gone around the circle twice, have everyone face toward the center of the circle again and discuss:

• *How does it feel knowing that people don't know everything about you?*

• *God says he* **does** *know everything about you. How does that feel?*

• *Would you rather your friends knew too little or too much about you? Why?*

Say: **One reason it's OK that God knows so much about us is that he also loves us. He knows the good things we do and the bad. He knows the good words we say and the bad. God knows us—and he cares for us, no matter what!**

Promise Kept BIBLE STORY

SHADOW SCRIPTURE

Time: about 15 minutes

Supplies: pencils, paper plates (1 per child), masking tape, safety scissors (1 pair per child), lamp (or flashlight), Bible

Say: **Considering how much God has on his mind—running the whole universe and everything!—it's easy to wonder if God keeps track of us all. Let's hear what the Bible says about that.**

Read aloud Psalm 139:1-4, 13; Matthew 10:29-31; John 3:16, 17. Say: **Seems as if God is making a couple of powerful promises: God knows you and loves you. Good to know!**

Ask kids to each cut a shape out of their paper plates that will remind them that God knows them and loves them. Read the Scripture passages again, if necessary. Say: **For instance, you might cut out the shape of a sparrow or two, or a hair, or a magnifying glass because God is always keeping us in sight. It's up to you—but please be finished in five minutes.**

Help kids tape their shapes to one end of their pencils (or skip taping to the pencils, if it would work better for your group to just hold their shapes). Darken the room a little, but don't turn off all the lights. Then take turns checking out the shapes as shadows on the wall. Let kids create shadows by holding the other end of the pencils as they place their shapes between the light and the wall.

Then, as a group, discuss:

▪ *Why did you cut out the shape you did? How does it remind you of God's promise to know us, love us, and care for us?*

▪ *In what ways does God show he knows you?*

▪ *In what ways does God show he loves and cares for you?*

Say: **God knows about what's happening in our lives, but he still wants us to talk to him about our lives. That's because God wants a friendship with us. He wants us to come to him. Let's do that now through prayer.**

CLOSING PRAYER

SHADOW PRAYER
Time: about 5 minutes
Supplies: lamp (or flashlight)

Ask kids to line up near the lamp. Say: **God knows about every hair on our heads. He knows every breath we take. Let's thank him for being so great that he can know and care about each of us—***and* **everyone else in the world. God is amazing!**

Ask kids to, one at a time, stand between the lamp and the wall so they can see their shadows. As each shadow is on the wall, pray for that child. Pray, **God, thank you for creating** (child's name) **to be a one-of-a-kind, special person. And thank you for loving him** (or her).

When you have prayed for each child, close by praying, **In Jesus' name, amen.**

EXTRA-TIME ACTIVITY—OPTION 1

I CARE BECAUSE

Time: about 10 minutes
Supplies: large bowl of water, paper towels

Ask kids to sit cross-legged on the floor in a circle. (Girls wearing skirts can sit on their knees.) Join them. Fill a large bowl—one that requires two hands to hold—nearly to the brim with water. It should be able to be passed without spilling, but barely.

Explain: **I'll pass the bowl to the person on my left, who will do the same, until the bowl returns to me. Then I'll send it the other direction.**

When you get the bowl a second time, place it carefully on the floor. If water has spilled, provide paper towels.

As a group, discuss:

- *Why did it matter if the water spilled? Or did it?*
- *Did you care more when it was over your lap? Why or why not?*

Say: **How much we care about something often has to do with how close we are to it. For instance, one of our friends getting sick usually matters more to us than if ten people we** *don't* **know get sick.**

Jesus cares about us—a lot. That's because he knows us . . . and because he loves us.

POP QUIZ

Time: about 10 minutes
Supplies: none

Put kids into same-age pairs. Explain that you'll call out an answer, and all children need to call out a question that fits the answer. Kids are competing with their partners—the first person in each pair to call out a good question wins. This is a think-fast game!

Possible answers might include: blue, a zebra, 42, spaghetti with broccoli balls, sandals, Godzilla, crackers, a lightbulb, the letter *L,* jellyfish, pink, John the Baptist, peach pits, daisies, fleas, oak trees, chicken lips, and a fish named Arthur. Add your own answers for more fun!

As a group, discuss:

- **What made this game easy or hard?**
- **We had to think of questions that fit with answers. God knows all the questions and all the answers already. What words would you use to describe God?**

INQUIRING MINDS WANT TO KNOW

Time: about 5 minutes
Supplies: none

Gather kids in a circle. Ask: **If God knows us and likes us, why do some people have trouble liking themselves?**

God's Promise
That It Will
All Work Out

The Point: When we love and follow God, we end up OK.
Scripture Connect: Romans 8:28, 31

Supplies for all Session 10 activities options: pencils, prepared poster, $1 bills (the crisper, the better; 1 per child and 1 for yourself; you decide if you want them back), Bible, 2-foot lengths of twine (1 per child and 1 for yourself), blindfold, movable furniture (if necessary)

The Basics for Leaders

"Relax—it's going to be OK."

That's the main idea of Romans 8:28. It's hard to hear when something has gone wrong, but for those who love and follow God, it's true. Things *will* be OK—because tough times can draw us closer to God, can help us rely more on God, and can show us God's love and power as God works in our lives.

So even if you have problems in your life, relax. It's going to be OK. *You're* going to be OK. The problems may be big—but God is bigger. If God is for you, who can be against you?

Love God. Follow God. And then watch God keep his awesome promise.

OPENING ACTIVITY—OPTION 1

HOWZITGOIN'

Time: about 5 minutes, depending on attendance
Supplies: pencils, prepared poster

Before kids arrive, draw a line on a poster. Place a 1 on the left end of the line, a 10 on the right, and a 5 in the middle. As kids arrive, ask them to pencil in their initials on the line.

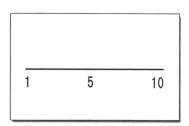

Say: **If this past week was so awful you wish you'd slept through it, place your initials by the 1. If it was a great week you wish you could repeat, put your initials by the 10. Place your initials anywhere on the line that shows how you feel about this past week—except exactly on the 5. That's because there's no such thing as a week that's exactly half good and half bad!**

After kids have signed in, give them 30 seconds each to explain why they placed their initials where they did. Be sure to include your own initials and explain your placement on the line. Kids will begin to express themselves more over time—and hearing their stories will help you adapt this lesson to make it relevant to your kids' lives.

OPENING ACTIVITY—OPTION 2

BASHED BILLS

Time: about 10 minutes
Supplies: $1 bills (the crisper, the better; 1 per child and 1 for yourself; you decide if you want them back)

Have everyone stand in a circle. Give each child a $1 bill and hold one yourself. Say: **Right now your $1 is worth 100 bright, shiny pennies. At least a few of these $1 bills are fresh and new—sort of like you used** to be. But you don't have to be around long before something happens that makes you feel less than good about yourself.

Fold your $1 bill in half. Say: **If you've ever felt bad about yourself after being chosen last for a team, or flunking a test, or if you've had people laugh at you for some reason, fold your $1 bill in half.**

Pause as kids fold their bills. Then say: **Sometimes we lose people or things we care about too. If you've ever lost someone or something you loved, crunch up your $1 bill like this.**

Roll up your $1 bill in a ball and pause as your kids do the same. Continue: **And sometimes people are mean to us for some reason. They bully us or say mean things. If that's happened to you, do this.**

Throw your $1 bill on the floor and step on it. Grind your heel on it. Pause as kids do the same.

Slowly pick up and unfold your $1 bill. Hold it up. Say: **This is looking worse all the time, isn't it? Open up your $1 bills too.**

Pause as kids do so. Ask: **How many pennies is your $1 bill worth now?**

Allow kids to answer: 100 pennies. Explain that, even folded, crumpled, and trampled, their $1 bills are still worth the same amount.

Have kids sit and, as a group, discuss:

▪ *There's an old saying: "Sticks and stones may break my bones, but words will never hurt me." What does that mean? Have you ever used that old saying?*

▪ *When people are mean or make fun of you, how do you feel? Why?*

▪ *Are you worth less when others point out your faults? Why do we often feel we're worth less?*

Say: **We all have tough days . . . or tough years. But even when others are mean to us, God still loves us. He still sent Jesus for us. God values you more highly than anything else in the universe. You've been made to last for eternity!**

That's why I can tell you that no matter what hard things you're facing now, or will face later, it's going to be OK. Love and follow God, and in the end, you'll be OK. That's God's promise.

If you choose to give the $1 bills to the kids, do so now. Tell them they're not to spend those dollars; they're to tape them up where they'll be a reminder that, no matter how hard the day, it's going to be OK. (Be sure and let parents know the kids have been given money.) If you choose to keep the $1 bills, ask for them back now.

Awesome Promise Game

Jump for It
Time: about 10 minutes
Supplies: none

Have kids line up, shoulder to shoulder. Explain that they're now standing on the very edge of a riverbank. On the bank are angry rattlesnakes that want to bite them. In the river in front of them are hungry piranhas that want the kids for lunch. But the rattlesnakes and piranhas can't attack at the same time, so if the kids will be in the river or on the bank at the right time, they're safe.

You'll shout out where kids should be. If you shout "river," they'll jump a few feet forward. If you shout "bank," they'll jump a few feet back.

Have fun. Shout out commands slowly, then quickly, and toss in fake-outs, such as "Ba . . . nks are the worst place to be right now" or "Ri . . . ght now piranhas are hungry, so stay out of the river."

After playing for a few minutes, have kids jump around on the bank, squishing rattlesnakes. Then have kids sit in a circle and, as a group, discuss:

- *What made this activity easy or hard?*

Say: **Sometimes if there are a lot of instructions, we have a hard time keeping up. That happened to me once when . . .**

Briefly share about a time that happened to you. Then say:

- *Your turn now. The speed of this activity made it hard. Is something happening with you these days that makes you wish you could speed up or that makes you feel like you can't keep up?*

When we love and follow God, things will turn out OK . . . but that doesn't mean you'll pass that math class or that your parents will quit fighting. God never says life will be easy. He says he'll walk

through our lives with us, if we ask him to, and that in the end all will be well. And that's a promise! Let's look at that awesome promise now.

Promise Kept BIBLE STORY

CATCH THIS!
Time: about 15 minutes
Supplies: Bible

Ask children to pair up. (Only one child showed up today? Join as his or her partner!) Partners should stand facing each other, about four feet apart. Ask children to each find two unbreakable things they brought with them, things that could be thrown or dropped without damage. A shoe, yes. A cell phone, no. Ask kids to hold the objects and then, gently, to begin tossing those objects to each other. The goal is to work together to keep as many of the objects going back and forth as possible—without dropping them—much as jugglers work together to keep objects in the air. One object is easy, two doable, three a challenge, and if a pair can keep four in the air . . . take a video and post it online—you've found future circus stars!

Allow several minutes of trying, and then have kids return objects to their owners and sit with you in a circle. As a group, discuss:

▪ *You had a lot of stuff coming at you at once! In a different way, you may feel like you have a lot of stuff coming at you with school, your family, chores, lessons, and activities. What—if anything—do you sometimes wish you could drop? Why?*

Read aloud Romans 8:28, 31.

▪ *Tell about a time it didn't feel like things were working out for your good. Maybe it was hearing that your parents were splitting up, or that your grandmother died. What happened to you that left you feeling like you might not be OK?*

After kids share, thank them. Read Romans 8:28, 31 aloud again. Say: **Those are powerful words. It's an awesome promise that no matter** what life throws at us, no matter how fast things come at us, God is with us. I'm glad that's true, but it doesn't always feel like it's true at the time. Let's talk to God about that.

CLOSING PRAYER

IT'S OK PRAYER

Time: about 5 minutes
Supplies: none

Ask kids to stand in a circle with you. Explain that you'll start the prayer by telling God about something that you're finding to be a challenge (difficult) right now. Invite kids to also share things that are challenging for them.

Then, when everyone has shared, pray: **God, you've promised that all things work together for good if we love and follow you and are doing what you want us to do. Help us follow you closely. Please work in and through us to make good things happen in our world—and in us. In Jesus' name, amen.**

EXTRA-TIME ACTIVITY—OPTION 1

KNOT ME

Time: about 10 minutes
Supplies: 2-foot lengths of twine (1 per child and 1 for yourself), Bible

Give each child a length of twine and a challenge: tie a knot without letting go of either end of the twine.

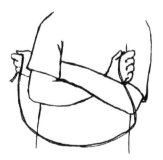

After they find they can't do it, cross your arms in front of your chest (as shown) and then grab an end of your length of twine in each hand. Uncross your arms, and you'll have a knot.

Ask kids to sit in a group. Say: **There was an**

easy answer to that problem—if you knew it. You needed details! God tells us to follow him, but doesn't always give all the details. For instance, Jesus says to love our enemies, people who hurt us (Matthew 5:44). **But how exactly do you do that? Jesus says to trust in him** (John 14:1), **but what does that look like at school?**

Discuss:

- **What's something you think God wants you to do—but you're not sure how to do it?**
- **What's something God wants you to do—but you haven't followed him and done it even if you know how?**

EXTRA-TIME ACTIVITY—OPTION 2

CAGE ESCAPE

Time: about 10 minutes
Supplies: blindfold, movable furniture (if necessary), Bible

Stand a volunteer in the center of the room. Have other kids circle up to form a "cage" around the volunteer. If you have just a few kids, have those kids stand apart, holding hands. Or use movable furniture to enlarge the circle. Your goal: create a closed circle with just one opening.

Explain that you'll blindfold the volunteer, spin him around several times, and the volunteer will then escape through the opening by following your voice. You'll stand just beyond the opening of the cage. The volunteer must walk out of the circle without bumping into anyone or anything.

Hold the volunteer by the shoulders as you spin him around. Then step outside the circle and call the volunteer to you.

Let kids all take turns being spun. Then have everyone be seated. Ask:

- **We know how to follow God because his voice speaks to us through the Bible. What do you find easy or hard about reading the Bible?**
- **How willing are you to follow God—even when you know you need to do something scary like telling someone about Jesus or meeting someone who's not like you?**

Say: **God is on our side. When we love and follow God, we end up OK. So let's follow God by doing what he says and going where he leads.**

EXTRA-TIME ACTIVITY—OPTION 3

INQUIRING MINDS WANT TO KNOW

Time: about 5 minutes
Supplies: none

Gather kids in a circle. Ask: ***If God promises we'll be OK in the end, why does he let us have problems at all?***

God's Promise
to Help Us
Stand Strong

The Point: We're not in this alone—God is with us.

Scripture Connect: 1 Corinthians 10:13; Ephesians 6:10-17

Supplies for all Session 11 activities options: pencils, prepared poster, several 2-page newspaper spreads, old magazines, safety scissors, glue, tape, paper (8½" x 14" or larger), Bible, 2" x 2" sticky notes (or paper squares; 5 per child), chair, index cards

The Basics for Leaders

It's easy to feel lonely. Even in a crowded classroom or bustling through a busy day, it's easy to wonder, *Does anyone really understand or care?*

But God's awesome promise is that we're not alone. God sees us. He knows the details of our lives. He wants to walk through our days with us and to help us stay close to him. We're only alone if we choose to be.

And we don't have to be beat up by temptations to stray from God—God provides the strength to fight temptation. He provides actual weapons, actual armor to protect us and help us to stand firm. And to win.

And that's a promise.

HOWZITGOIN'

Time: about 5 minutes, depending on attendance
Supplies: pencils, prepared poster

Before kids arrive, draw a line on a poster. Place a 1 on the left end of the line, a 10 on the right, and a 5 in the middle. As kids arrive, ask them to pencil in their initials on the line.

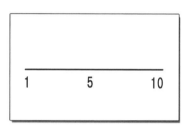

Say: **If this past week was so awful you wish you'd slept through it, place your initials by the 1. If it was a great week you wish you could repeat, put your initials by the 10. Place your initials anywhere on the line that shows how you feel about this past week—except exactly on the 5. That's because there's no such thing as a week that's exactly half good and half bad!**

After kids have signed in, give them 30 seconds each to explain why they placed their initials where they did. Be sure to include your own initials and explain your placement on the line. Kids will begin to express themselves more over time—and hearing their stories will help you adapt this lesson to make it relevant to your kids' lives.

WELCOME TO THE CLUB!

Time: about 10 minutes
Supplies: none

Have children stand and mingle in an open area. Explain that you'll call out categories and then count down from 10 seconds as they find others who share the same characteristics in that category. For instance, if you call out "types of pets," the cat owners must find other cat owners, and dog owners find other dog owners—quickly!

Categories you might use include: left- or right-handed, eye color, number of brothers and sisters, number of pets, favorite flavor of ice cream, birthday month, least favorite subject in school. (Note: For extra fun—and risk!—ask children to call out their own categories.)

Then use as the final category: people God loves. That should include everyone, so join that group yourself. Then have kids sit on the floor. Discuss:

• **Did any of you end up all alone in a category? Were you glad or sad about that?** Briefly tell about a category you're in that others in the room probably aren't in. Maybe you're married or a high school student or speak French.

• **How do you feel when you find yourself all alone in a place where everyone else seems to know each other? For instance, if you're the new kid in class.**

• **Tell about a time you felt like the only person who wanted to obey Jesus. Maybe your buddies wanted to do something that you knew you shouldn't do. What happened?**

Say: **God has promised he's always with us—and he'll give us the power to stand firm for him. We'll find out more about that in a few minutes!**

Awesome Promise Game

Bigfoot
Time: about 10 minutes
Supplies: several 2-page newspaper spreads

Open a newspaper spread on the floor. Explain that the goal of this game is for your entire group to stand on the paper. If you have just a few kids, it will be easy. If you have a lot of kids, they'll have to be creative to get everyone on the spread with nobody off the edges. (Note: If your group is really large, divide into doable numbers and give each smaller group a newspaper spread.)

After successfully fitting on that spread, fold the paper in half and have kids again all squeeze on. Keep folding the paper until all fitting on it becomes impossible.

Have kids sit and, as a group, discuss:

- **What did you try that helped you fit on the paper?**
- **Tell about another time you were squished in a tight space. Where were you, and what were you doing?**
- **You stood strong in this activity, but when we folded the paper one time too many, we couldn't all fit. What's something you think you could never do, no matter how hard you tried?**
- **We want to live in a way that pleases God, but we do things we shouldn't do. We say things we shouldn't say. No matter how hard we try, we aren't perfect. What can we do—if anything—to always live in a way that pleases God?**

Say: **God wants us to live in a way that pleases him, but God knows we don't always obey him. God wants us to stand strong for him, and he's willing to help us stand strong. Let's find out more about that!**

Promise Kept BIBLE STORY

THAT'S ME!

Time: about 15 minutes

Supplies: old magazines, safety scissors, glue, tape, paper (8½" x 14" or larger), Bible, 2" x 2" sticky notes (or paper squares; 5 per child)

Give each child a sheet of paper. Scatter the magazines, scissors, glue, and tape on the floor or work table so they're easy for kids to reach.

Explain that a collage is a collection of words and pictures. Ask kids to create a collage of their daily lives. They can choose from the magazines any pictures and words that represent people they know, activities they enjoy, and places they go.

Allow up to eight minutes for kids to create their collages. When time is up, ask kids to form trios (they'll remain in their trios for the rest of this activity) and show their collages to their small group, explaining why they selected the words and pictures they selected.

Say: **Thanks for sharing! Your collage shows how you live. It also shows places where you may be tempted to do wrong things. We sometimes give in to temptation and make bad choices, choices that don't please God. For instance . . .**

Briefly share about a place where you're tempted to do wrong. For instance, you might say, **"When I'm at work, I'm often tired. I'm tempted to be angry and say things I shouldn't say."** Sharing your own story will help kids know what sort of response you want. Then have trios discuss:

• *What wrong things are you tempted to do in the places shown on your collage?*

Allow time for the discussion and then distribute sticky notes to each child. Say: **God promises to help us be strong.** Read 1 Corinthians 10:13. Then say: **He gives us weapons that help us do battle with temptation— and win. As I read a list of the weapons—the armor of God—look at your collage. Whenever you hear a weapon that would help you beat temptation to do wrong things somewhere shown on your collage, place a sticky note over that picture or word.**

Read aloud Ephesians 6:10-17, pausing after each piece of armor listed so kids can interact with their collages:

- belt of truth (being truthful)
- body armor of God's righteousness (deciding to do what God says is right)
- shoes of peace (being prepared by knowing and following Jesus)
- shield of faith (having faith in God)
- helmet of salvation (having hope in God)
- sword of the Spirit (knowing God's Word and sharing it with others)

Say: **I'm so glad God promised that no temptation will be too big to stand up against, if we let him help us . . . and if we do the things he told us to do to get ready. Let's thank God for that!**

(Note: You'll need the collages for the Chair Prayer activity.)

CLOSING PRAYER

CHAIR PRAYER

Time: about 5 minutes
Supplies: collages from the That's Me! activity, chair

Have the collages from the That's Me! activity nearby. Place a chair in the middle of the room and gather children around it. Explain that for your prayer time together, you'll take turns sitting in the chair. The only person who can talk will be the person seated, and that person will be thanking God for being with us in tough times of temptation.

Begin by being seated yourself. Thank God for his love and for being with you in the place you mentioned earlier, the place you're tempted to do wrong.

After those kids who want to pray have done so, ask everyone to place their collages on the seat of the chair and finish by praying as follows: **God, we give you our lives. We thank you for the promise that you are with us in every situation, every moment, every day—wherever we are. In Jesus' name, amen.**

EXTRA-TIME ACTIVITY—OPTION 1

HANDY—OR NOT?

Time: about 10 minutes
Supplies: pencils, index cards

Give each child a pencil and an index card. Say: **I want you each to hold the card and write or print your name on it. Easy, right? Except you can only use one hand to hold the card and write on it. And the card can't touch anything except that one hand. Give it a try.**

Allow time and then, as a group, discuss:

▪ *How much easier would this have been if you'd had a second hand to help you? Why?*

▪ *What was a tough time in your life when having God's help would have made things easier?*

Say: **God is with you—and God will help you stand strong and deal with temptations and troubles. But you've got to be willing to obey him and strap on the armor he's provided to help you. Are you willing?**

EXTRA-TIME ACTIVITY—OPTION 2

ARMS RACE

Time: about 10 minutes
Supplies: none

Have kids pair up and stand, facing you. Explain that you'll all exercise together. Say: **Hold your right arm straight up above your head and say "One." Now drop your right arm straight down to your side and say "Two." Move your arm up and down as I say "One, two, one, two."**

Have kids repeat the series ten times so it becomes routine.

Now hold your left arm straight over your head and say "One." Move your left arm straight out from your shoulder and say "Two." Now drop your left arm down to your side and say "Three." Move your left arm up, straight out, and down as I say "One, two, three, one, two, three."

Repeat ten times.

Now use both arms and hold them in the correct positions—at the same time!—as I call out numbers.

Start with "One," and then randomly call out either "One," "Two," or "Three" to put kids through their paces. It's confusing! After a minute or so, have kids sit and, as a group, discuss:

- *What made this activity easy or hard?*
- *Why is following directions sometimes harder than it looks?*
- *Why is following God's directions sometimes harder than it looks?*

Say: **Good news! God will help us follow his directions for our lives even when things are hard. God will help us stand strong—if we'll let him. It's an awesome promise.**

INQUIRING MINDS WANT TO KNOW

Time: about 5 minutes
Supplies: none

Ask: **God wants us to stand strong and believe. What makes it hard for you to believe that God will help you?**

God's Promise
That There's
Nothing to Fear

The Point: We don't need to be afraid.
Scripture Connect: Isaiah 46:9; Philippians 4:13; 1 John 4:4

Supplies for all Session 12 activities options: pencils, prepared poster, card stock (or construction paper), markers, safety scissors, masking tape, Bible, shallow basket (or bowl), paper

The Basics for Leaders

Even the bravest people you know are afraid of something . . . or someone. The dark. Spiders. Surprise quizzes. Bullies . . .

But God's awesome promise is that there's no need to live in fear. Not that it's wrong to *feel* fear—that's just being human—but we don't need to be *ruled* by fear. Because even though the world is full of scary stuff, we're in good hands. We're in God's hands, and God is greater than anything we could fear.

God never promises to protect us from loss, pain, death . . . or surprise quizzes. But he does promise that what we fear is temporary, and that life with him is now and forever.

So live boldly! The all-powerful, eternal, one-and-only God is with you and has already won the battle.

There's nothing to fear!

HOWZITGOIN'

Time: about 5 minutes, depending on attendance
Supplies: pencils, prepared poster

Before kids arrive, draw a line on a poster. Place a 1 on the left end of the line, a 10 on the right, and a 5 in the middle. As kids arrive, ask them to pencil in their initials on the line.

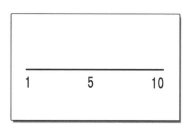

Say: **If this past week was so awful you wish you'd slept through it, place your initials by the 1. If it was a great week you wish you could repeat, put your initials by the 10. Place your initials anywhere on the line that shows how you feel about this past week—except exactly on the 5. That's because there's no such thing as a week that's exactly half good and half bad!**

After kids have signed in, give them 30 seconds each to explain why they placed their initials where they did. Be sure to include your own initials and explain your placement on the line. Kids will begin to express themselves more over time—and hearing their stories will help you adapt this lesson to make it relevant to your kids' lives.

FEAR FACE

Time: about 10 minutes
Supplies: none

Ask children to sit on the floor in pairs, facing each other. Explain that you'll call out a number of things that frighten people. Kids are to show how much each thing scares them by making a fear face. If it scares them a lot, they'll make a full-out, eyes bulging face and scream (if that won't disturb others nearby). If the thing you call out doesn't scare them at all, they'll yawn.

Have kids practice making faces of both extremes—screaming face and yawning face.

Say: **You can make either of those faces or a face in between. You decide, based on how much these things scare you.**

You can add to the list, but include these:

▪ spiders	▪ death	▪ rattlesnakes
▪ clowns	▪ dogs	▪ dentists
▪ being in small spaces	▪ doctors	▪ needles
▪ the dark	▪ being left out	▪ water
▪ singing in front of people	▪ flowers	▪ falling
	▪ bats	▪ germs
▪ heights	▪ moths	▪ me

When finished, have kids sit in a circle and, as a group, discuss:

▪ *Why do you think you're afraid of those things?*

▪ *What do you do when you're scared? Do you scream, get quiet, or do something else?*

▪ *Tell about a time someone else was afraid but you weren't.*

Say: **When I get scared, I like to have someone with me who isn't scared, who can take care of things. Good news: we all have someone like that! It's God—and God says we don't have to be afraid, because he's with us.**

We'll dig into that more, but first let's play a game I call Falling for You!

Awesome Promise Game

Falling for You
Time: about 10 minutes
Supplies: none

(Note: Safety first! You know your group. Adapt this activity if there's any risk of injury.)

Have kids pair up. Be sure kids in each pair are about the same size and are the same sex, if possible. Have kids in each pair stand, one child behind the other. Each child in the rear should be about two feet behind the child in front.

Explain that, on your signal, the child in front will raise his or her arms slightly so that the child behind can slip his or her arms beneath the arms of the child in front when the child in front falls backwards. But only on your signal!

Demonstrate with a volunteer so kids know how to catch each other.

Say: **If you're in front, close your eyes and raise your arms slightly. Straighten your legs, and when I give you the word—and not before—just tip over backwards. Your partner will—I hope!—catch you. But you don't really know, do you? Let's give it a try. Tip now.**

Some children will tip back readily. Some may not be able to bring themselves to do it; don't force them.

Have partners change places. After each child has both tipped backwards and caught a partner, have kids circle up and discuss:

- *Which did you like best, tipping or catching? Why?*

- *How did it feel when you felt yourself falling backwards—scary or fun?*

- *You knew someone would catch you just now. But what if you weren't sure you'd be caught? Would you still be able to fall backwards? Why or why not?*

Say: **Lots of people say, "Don't be scared." Moms, dads, swimming instructors, dentists, teachers . . . But for that to work, you have to trust the person telling you there's nothing to fear. And you have to believe the person will help you! God promises us that there's nothing to fear and that he'll help us. Let's find out more about that now!**

Promise Kept BIBLE STORY

FEAR MASKS

Time: about 15 minutes

Supplies: card stock (or construction paper), markers, safety scissors, masking tape, Bible

Give each child a sheet of card stock and a marker. Say: **Everyone is afraid of something, but we're not afraid of the same things. We found that out playing Fear Face! As for me, I'm afraid of . . .**

Briefly share about a fear. Doing so will help kids feel more comfortable sharing their fears.

Say: **Please draw a mask that represents what you're afraid of. Maybe it's something we talked about earlier, or maybe it isn't. Either way, find a way to draw it on your mask. For instance, if you're afraid of water, you might draw goggles. If you're afraid of heights, you might draw a mask that has clouds on it. You'll cut out the mask and wear it, so put eyeholes in it!**

After kids have created their masks, prepare the masks so the kids can wear them. You'll make "string" out of masking tape. Each mask needs two long strips of tape cut the same length. Attach the top portion of a mask to the center of the first piece of tape. Then back that piece of tape with the other piece. Repeat for all the masks and help tie the masks on the kids' heads. Have kids take turns sharing what their masks represent and continue to wear their masks as you read aloud Philippians 4:13 and 1 John 4:4.

> **AGE-ALERT TIPS**
>
> Kids of **all ages** probably will need help cutting the eyeholes.

Masks still on, discuss together:

▪ **What's something you used to be afraid of, but now you don't fear it?**

▪ **What happened so you were not afraid any longer?**

▪ **What do you think it will take for you to get over the fear you've** *drawn on your mask?*

Say: **Just telling ourselves not to be afraid usually doesn't work. We need help overcoming our fears, and I know where we can go to find help.**

Have kids keep wearing their masks as they move into the De-Mask Prayers activity.

CLOSING PRAYER

DE-MASK PRAYERS

Time: about 5 minutes
Supplies: masks from Fear Mask activity, shallow basket (or bowl)

Kids should be wearing their masks from the Fear Mask activity. Place the basket where kids can easily see it. Say: **It's not wrong to sometimes feel afraid. That's just natural. But if fear is keeping you awake at night, that's not good. And because God is greater than anything or anyone you might be afraid of, it's not necessary!**

God said, "I am God, and there is none like me" (Isaiah 46:9). **We can give our fears to God, who is bigger and stronger than anything that frightens us. Please take off your masks. If you're ready to let God help you with your fears, put your mask in this basket.**

Pause to allow kids time to respond, if they want to do so.

Pray: **God, thank you that you're stronger than anything and anyone. Help us remember that you're with us—always. And help us remember that you've already won every battle and beaten everything that causes us to be afraid. In Jesus' name, amen.**

(Note: If you're doing more activities, lay the masks aside until it's time for the kids to take them home.)

EXTRA-TIME ACTIVITY—OPTION 1

FEAR-FREE ZONE

Time: about 10 minutes
Supplies: paper, markers, safety scissors

Ask children to create "Fear-Free Zone" signs to place where they experience fear. That may be at school where they're bullied, or in their rooms where they find it hard to sleep because they're afraid of the dark.

Explain that they can design any sort of sign they wish—but they'll be asked to show it to others and explain where they plan to hang it.

Allow time for kids to make their signs, and then ask each child to take a turn showing his or her sign and explaining where it will be placed.

Say: **I'm glad that God will help us not to be afraid. He's said there's nothing to fear because, in the end, if we love and follow him, we'll be with him forever. That's good news!**

EXTRA-TIME ACTIVITY—OPTION 2

LIVE BOLDLY

Time: about 10 minutes
Supplies: none

Say: **Someone who's not afraid of heights and water will climb up to the high diving board. A bold (brave) person will do more—he'll jump off.**

The Bible is full of bold people who jumped into trusting God. David went out to fight the giant Goliath. Moses went to Egypt to talk to Pharaoh. Peter preached about Jesus even when he was in danger.

We can be brave too. We can live boldly in serving God.

As a group, discuss:

▪ *Tell about a time you did something bold. What was it—and how did it turn out?*

▪ *What bold thing do you think God might want you to do? What's stopping you from doing it?*

EXTRA-TIME ACTIVITY—OPTION 3

INQUIRING MINDS WANT TO KNOW

Time: about 5 minutes
Supplies: none

Gather kids in a circle. Ask: **The Bible talks about fearing God. For example, Psalm 34:11 says, "I will teach you to fear the LORD." Does this mean we should be scared of God, or might it mean something else?**

God's Promise
of Eternal
Life

The Point: We can live with Jesus in Heaven—forever.
Scripture Connect: John 14:2, 3; Romans 6:23; 10:9

Supplies for all Session 13 activities options: pencils, prepared poster, playing cards (or index cards; at least 10 per child), Bibles, tray with 24 items on it and a towel to cover, paper, adhesive bandages (1 per child), pens

The Basics for Leaders

It's a promise written in almost every yearbook: "Best Friends Forever!"

And maybe the people who promise "BFF" mean it—but life gets in the way. Friends move. They go to different schools. Their interests change. They find new best friends. And before you know it, "BFF" stands for "Best Fickle Friend."

Maybe you've experienced that people who promised to be there for you forever just sort of faded away. The friendship slowly disappeared.

That's not going to happen with God. When he promises to be a friend forever, he means forever. God really is the best friend who'll never give up on you—and he proved it. He gave his Son, Jesus, for you. And Jesus has prepared an eternal home for you.

In this session you'll be helping your kids understand God's awesome promise that we can live with him in Heaven—forever.

OPENING ACTIVITY—OPTION 1

HOWZITGOIN'
Time: about 5 minutes, depending on attendance
Supplies: pencils, prepared poster

Before kids arrive, draw a line on a poster. Place a 1 on the left end of the line, a 10 on the right, and a 5 in the middle. As kids arrive, ask them to pencil in their initials on the line.

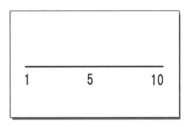

Say: **If this past week was so awful you wish you'd slept through it, place your initials by the 1. If it was a great week you wish you could repeat, put your initials by the 10. Place your initials anywhere on the line that shows how you feel about this past week—except exactly on the 5. That's because there's no such thing as a week that's exactly half good and half bad!**

After kids have signed in, give them 30 seconds each to explain why they placed their initials where they did. Be sure to include your own initials and explain your placement on the line. Kids will begin to express themselves more over time—and hearing their stories will help you adapt this lesson to make it relevant to your kids' lives.

OPENING ACTIVITY—OPTION 2

GETTING IN
Time: about 10 minutes
Supplies: none

Ask children to sit on the floor in a circle. Join them. Say: **Let's pretend we're in a secret club—one that needs a signal so others know who's in the club.**

Place your left index finger behind your left ear. Say: **If this were our** signal, I could do this as I walked into a room and other club members would know that I was in the club. Maybe this isn't the best signal. Who else has an idea?

After kids share their ideas, have the group vote to adopt a specific signal. Practice it several times. As a group, discuss:

• *Tell about a club or group you've joined. Maybe it was the Cub Scouts or Brownies, or a sports team. How do those group members know who else is in the group? And why did you join?*

If I could join any group—a team, a band, or any other group—I'd want to join . . .

Briefly tell about a group you'd like to join (have fun—join the Beatles or the cast of your favorite movie!). And tell why. Sharing your story models the sort of story you'd like your kids to share. It also helps them get to know you better. Say:

• *Your turn now. Tell about a group you'd like to join.*

After kids share, continue: **Today we'll talk about a group we can all join: the Eternal Lifers. God has promised that anyone who loves Jesus—who accepts and follows Jesus—can have eternal life and spend all that time with him.** Ask:

• *What—if anything—is a sign that someone's in that group? How can you tell who's in and who's not?*

• *Before we go to Heaven, what's the best thing about being in the Eternal Lifers?*

Say: **The Eternal Lifers is a group I want to be in! Let's talk about it some more.**

Awesome Promise Game

Coolest Place Ever
Time: about 10 minutes
Supplies: playing cards (or index cards; at least 10 per child), Bibles

Group children into trios and have them sit on the floor.

Say: **Even if you live in a great place, there's probably something you'd change to turn it into the coolest place ever. Maybe you'd add a game room. Or a pool. Or a racetrack! In your trio, talk about this:**

• What—if anything—would you change about where you live to turn it into the coolest place ever?

Ask kids to report to the big group what they talked about in their trios. Then give each child at least ten playing cards.

AGE-ALERT TIPS

If you have **young children,** group them with **older kids** for this activity.

Say: **With your trio, make a house out of your cards. You can't bend, stick, or roll cards, but you can lean them against each other or stack them. See how close you can come to making a scale model of the coolest place ever!**

After several minutes, have kids check out other trios' houses.

Say: **Even the coolest house here is probably not quite the coolest place ever. But you can live in the coolest place ever. The Bible says that those who accept and follow Jesus get to be with him in Heaven—forever.**

Have some older children read aloud John 14:2, 3; Romans 6:23; and 10:9. Say: **Eternal life—that's an awesome promise! Let's find out more about God's promise!**

Promise Kept BIBLE STORY

IT'S ALL ABOUT JESUS

Time: about 15 minutes
Supplies: tray with 24 items on it and a towel to cover, pencils, paper, Bible

Beforehand, prepare a tray with 24 items. Cover the items with a towel, and place the tray out of sight before the kids arrive. Some possible items for the tray: pen or other desk items, candy, envelope, kitchen utensils, spool of thread, mirror, toilet paper, and a few unusual items (such as foreign coins, tiny springs from inside ballpoint pens).

Ask kids to sit in a row. Give each child sheet of paper and a pencil. Say: **One way people join clubs is to pass a test. Sometimes it's a memory test. Let's see how good your memories are. Pay close attention to me as I show you some items.**

Explain that you'll show children a tray containing 24 items. Kids can't touch the tray or write down items until you give them the signal. As you walk past each child, have your left eye closed, but don't draw attention to this fact. After slowly walking past each child with the tray, place the towel over the tray again, and give children two minutes to list or draw every item on the tray.

As kids work on their lists, step away and change small details about your appearance. Add a hair clip, put a pen in your pocket, move a ring to an unusual finger, or add or remove glasses.

After two minutes, have kids call out the items they wrote down. Depending on your group, you could suggest that kids combine lists to see if, together, they can recall all 24 items. When they're done, remove the towel and let kids see the items again. Then ask:

• *When I passed the tray, did I have both my eyes open? If not, which eye was closed?*

• *What's changed about my appearance since I first showed you the tray?*

• *I told you to pay close attention to me as I showed you some items. Why didn't you notice me during this activity?*

Say: **Paying attention isn't worth much if we focus on the wrong things. I'm glad you remembered the items on the tray, but I'd asked you to pay close attention to *me*.**

Briefly tell about a time you focused on the wrong thing; for example, a time in school when you studied the wrong material for a test. Share the sort of answer you hope to hear from kids. Then say:

• *Your turn. What's a time you paid attention to the wrong person or thing? Maybe you didn't listen as a parent gave you a chore to do and you did the wrong chore. Or maybe you read the wrong chapter for your homework.*

After kids share their stories, thank them.

Say: **When people want to get into the Eternal Lifers club, they sometimes focus on doing good deeds. Maybe they go to church every Sunday and memorize lots of Bible verses. Those are good things to do—but God gives us eternal life as a gift. We can't earn it by doing a list of good deeds. When we believe that God raised Jesus from the dead, believe that "Jesus is Lord," we can decide to love and obey him. Let's pay attention to Jesus, and let's take him up on his awesome promise of eternal life!**

CLOSING PRAYER

BANDAGE PRAYER

Time: about 5 minutes
Supplies: adhesive bandages (1 per child)

Give each child an adhesive bandage. Say: **Jesus wants us to follow and obey him, but sometimes things get in the way. For instance, maybe you get angry easily and say mean things. Or you go places you shouldn't go. Whatever gets in the way of your following Jesus, let's ask for his help with that.**

Explain that kids (and you) will each open a bandage and place it on a part of your bodies that symbolizes your areas of difficulty. For example, if *going* to wrong places is a problem, put the bandage on a foot. If *thinking* mean thoughts, on the forehead.

Ask kids to open their bandages and hold them in their hands. Then pray: **God, please show us what is keeping us from following Jesus more closely. What do you want to change in us so we can better follow Jesus?**

Pause, and then ask kids to place their bandages on their bodies.

Pray: **God, thank you for your promise of making a place for us to live with you in Heaven—forever. Thank you for loving us and helping us change. We want to please you, God. In Jesus' name, amen.**

EXTRA-TIME ACTIVITY—OPTION 1

SILLY WALK CONGA LINE
Time: about 10 minutes
Supplies: none

Ask kids to stand and line up, single file. And then to each place their hands on the waist of the child in front of them. Join them. Have kids take turns leading the group as it walks around the room. The goal: for the child in front to do some sort of silly walk that others in the line will do behind the leader.

After everyone has led, have kids sit and discuss:

- *Who was the silliest leader? Why do you answer as you do?*
- *Who was the calmest leader? Why do you answer as you do?*
- *How do we know how to follow Jesus?*

Say: **Those who know, love, and follow Jesus have him as a leader—forever!**

EXTRA-TIME ACTIVITY—OPTION 2

SKETCHY SKETCHES
Time: about 10 minutes
Supplies: paper, pens, Bible

Distribute paper and pens. Ask kids to find partners and sit back-to-back. Ask the older child in each pair to draw a simple picture and describe it to his or her partner—without naming what's in the drawing. For instance, a house could be described as "a square with a triangle on top." The partner in each pair will draw the picture according to the description he's hearing—without seeing the original.

Have kids in each pair compare pictures. Then do the activity again with the younger child describing what to draw.

Have a few pairs show the larger group their pictures. As a group, discuss:

- *What made this activity easy or hard?*
- *Which did you like most: drawing the picture or describing it?*

Say: **Jesus' follower John said, in Revelation 21, that Heaven was like a city. He said it was "a square"** (v. 16), **it was "pure gold, as clear as glass"** (v. 18), **it had "twelve gates"** (v. 21), **and that there was "no night" there** (v. 25).

- *John described Heaven for us—but we can't see it ourselves until we get there. How is that like this activity?*
- *What are you looking forward to in Heaven? Why?*

EXTRA-TIME ACTIVITY—OPTION 3

INQUIRING MINDS WANT TO KNOW
Time: about 5 minutes
Supplies: none

Gather kids in a circle. Ask: ***Since you're going to be in Heaven a very long time, what can you do now to get ready for Heaven?***

About the **Author**

Mikal Keefer has published more than twenty books and is a frequent contributor to Group Publishing curriculum. He is an active children's ministry volunteer in his local church in Loveland, Colorado. He and his wife have led and participated in small groups for decades—except when their children were young and there were no resources to use with the kids while the adult small group was underway. At last those resources exist . . . just in time for his grandkids!

Mikal is the author of the other books in this series:
- *13 Very Bad Days and How God Fixed Them*
- *13 Very Cool Stories and Why Jesus Told Them*
- *13 Very Big Mistakes and What God Did About Them*

These **Standard Publishing**
resources will add even
more **fun** to each **session!**

Session 1—His People
Canyon Rescue! Item # 04731
Proverbs 3:5 (stickers) Item # 43245

Session 2—Noah
Noah's Rainbow Race Board Game
Item # 02906
Rainbow Miniatures (stickers)
Item # 43156

Session 3—Abram
Abraham Trusts God Happy Day® Book
Item # 023800509
What Is Faith? Happy Day® Book
Item # 02990

Session 4—David
*Jesus Is Born Happy Day® Coloring
Book* Item # 37058
Modern Hearts (stickers) Item # 43122

Session 5—a Savior
*The Best Thing About Christmas Happy
Day® Book* Item # 04362
Christmas Item # 04007

Session 6—Zechariah and Elizabeth
Mini Bibles (stickers) Item # 43241

Session 7—a Woman in Pain
Psalm 9:1 (stickers) Item # 01460
Prayer (stickers) Item # 01452

Session 8—to Rise from the Dead
Celebrate Jesus! Happy Day® Book
Item # 37038
Jesus Died and Lives (stickers)
Item # 01213

Session 9—to See and Love Us
Jesus & Children (stickers) Item # 43168
Psalm 139:14 (stickers) Item # 01229

Session 10—It Will All Work Out
*Count My Blessings Happy Day® Color-
ing Book* Item # 37019
God Cares for Claire Item # 04012

Session 11—to Help Us Stand Strong
*Armor of God Happy Day® Coloring
Book* (with stickers) Item # 37027
The Armor of God Item # 04727
Armor of God Board Game Item # 02909

Session 12—There's Nothing to Fear
Heroes Item # 04040
*Old Testament Faith Heroes Happy Day®
Book* Item # 021522810
Old Testament Heroes (stickers)
Item # 01215
Keep Trying, Travis! Happy Day® Book
Item # 04170

Session 13—Eternal Life
My Story of Jesus Happy Day® Book
Item # 04176
Will I See You Today? Item # 025444451
Happy Stars (stickers) Item # 43141

Teacher Resources
The Young Reader's Bible Item # 04871
Bible Puzzles for Kids (Ages 6–8)
Item # 02260
Bible Crafts & More (Ages 6–8)
Item # 02275
Bible Stories to Color & Tell
Item # 02492
Thru-the-Bible Coloring Pages (Ages
6–8) Item # 02274
Through the Bible Puzzles for Kids 8–12
Item # 02726
Don't Mess with Moses Item # 04870
Zack, You're Acting Zany
Item # 020474310

Available at your local Christian bookstore
or Standard Publishing at 1-800-543-1353
or www.standardpub.com

Standard
P U B L I S H I N G
Bringing The Word to Life

standardpub.com